Environmental Noise Barriers

Environmental Noise Barriers

A Guide to their Acoustic and
Visual Design

Benz Kotzen and Colin English

E & FN SPON
An Imprint of Routledge
London and New York

First published 1999
by E & FN Spon, an imprint of Routledge
11 New Fetter Lane, London EC4P 4EE

Simultaneously published in the USA and Canada
by Routledge
29 West 35th Street, New York, NY10001

© 1999 Benz Kotzen and Colin English

Typeset in Goudy
by Keystroke, Jacaranda Lodge, Wolverhampton
Printed and bound in China

British Library Cataloguing in Publication Data
A catalogue record for this book is available from the British Library

Library of Congress Cataloging in Publication Data
A catalogue record for this book has been requested

ISBN 0–419–23180–3

Contents

Preface

The genesis of this book was a jointly written conference paper titled 'Integrating European Scale Barriers into the English Landscape'. As we struggled to condense the material to fit a 40 minute slot, one of us rashly suggested that it might be easier to expand it into a book. Throughout this project we have been sustained by a desire to see an improvement in the current standard of practice in the control of road and rail noise in the UK and to ensure that those whose lives are afflicted by excessive traffic noise may enjoy a less stressful and more tranquil environment.

Work began on the project in the early 1990s. At that time the UK Government was pursuing a major roads programme which included the construction of many new bypasses and extensive motorway widening schemes. It became clear to us as we worked on some of these schemes, however, that the full noise implications were not being addressed. These roads were being designed to carry far greater volumes of traffic than had previously been the case, but the measures in use at that time were an inadequate solution to control the resultant noise. Taller and taller wooden fences did not offer a satisfactory solution to the noise problem; moreover, they would be an eyesore.

We had to look outside the UK to find more acceptable solutions to the problem. It soon became apparent that in certain European countries, although barriers were being used along roads to control traffic noise, these were quite different in specification to those in use in the UK. We were impressed, too, by the variety of barriers in use, many of them visually striking. We felt that it was important to research terrestrial transport noise control methods in Europe and elsewhere, and ask key questions. Could similar barriers be employed in the UK? Why is the use of sound-absorptive barriers widespread abroad and seldom considered in the UK? Why are some barriers visually acceptable while others offend the eye?

All too often in the UK, the impression is given that barriers are not properly planned and designed. Good design should involve acoustic engineers and landscape architects who may have conflicting priorities. Accordingly, we have set out to examine both acoustic and landscape issues, to give guidance on good practice and to highlight the pitfalls of bad design.

The Department of Transport issues guidance for its own road designers on how to plan, design and build barriers, and this can also be followed by those building barriers on local roads and railways. This book is intended to supplement that advice. We want to show the variety of solutions which can be achieved in different locations. To do this we have included as many photographs and illustrations as possible, not so that these designs can simply be copied, but to serve as a resource and stimulus in future noise barrier design.

Environmental noise pollution is a problem that is being addressed with increasing seriousness in many countries in continental Europe. The UK has much to learn from these countries about noise control policies and their implementation, because their solutions offer variety and ingenuity of design. These studies have taken us to Belgium, Denmark, France, Germany, the Netherlands, Italy and Switzerland in order to examine the wealth of barriers devised for different acoustic and landscape situations in these countries. We have, of course, met many transport industry officials and planners during our travels and been impressed by their sense of social responsibility and their commitment to the task of providing a better acoustic and visual environment for their citizens. Moreover, during meetings with continental barrier manufacturers, we have been encouraged to learn that most have close links with manufacturers and suppliers in this country who offer the same products and expertise. This will allow similar solutions to be readily implemented here.

Sadly, short-term solutions and cost cutting tend to dog road planning in the UK. A recently constructed road scheme has cost the Government more in compensation payments to local residents for the depreciation caused to their property, than the original cost of building the road. It is true that since we started work on this book the scale of the roads programme has been reduced considerably; the need for larger, better designed barriers has not diminished, however. The public, increasingly well-informed about the problem of excessive noise, is no longer prepared to tolerate a noisy environment. Compensation costs will continue to grow unless and until the impact of traffic noise is reduced.

Furthermore, the reduction of noise on existing roads is long overdue. The very high noise levels endured by so many people living alongside established roads is becoming intolerable. Many of these roads now carry far more traffic than was ever anticipated. We should follow the example of many other European countries by recognising the damaging social and health effects caused by such exposure and implementing noise control programmes on our busier roads.

Our original purpose in writing this book was to create a source book for all those involved in the design of barriers in the UK. We felt, too, that they would be interested in our investigation of the background reasons for the slower development of UK barrier design compared with elsewhere. Nevertheless, we hope that, as the design principles in this book have universal application, this book will also be of use to barrier designers outside the UK.

It is possible to control terrestrial transportation noise, and to improve the appearance of the necessary barriers. There are many examples of this in Europe and elsewhere; more recently, there have been some encouraging developments in the design and provision in the UK. We hope that this book helps to stimulate debate on the better protection of those affected by traffic noise and acts as a catalyst for the design and implementation of successful barriers.

Benz Kotzen and Colin English,
July 1998

Acknowledgements

We are grateful to many people, companies and organisations who have so willingly shared their time, knowledge and expertise with us, and to those who have been supportive in the endeavour to improve the quality and character of noise barriers and the control of traffic noise in the UK.

Thanks are due to the Rees Jeffrys Road Fund and Arup Acoustics, for without their generous support it would not have been possible to carry out much of the research needed for this book. Thanks are due also to the Rees Jeffreys Road Fund and the Brian Large Trust whose generosity made it possible to include fully integrated colour illustrations in the book.

We are indebted to the following people and organisations for their time in meetings and on field trips: Christo Padmos and Wynand Kooring of the Ministry of Transport, Public Works and Water Management, Delft and Rotterdam, the Netherlands; Brian Hunibell of the Environmental Noise Barrier Association, England; Mr Komsthof of the Freie und Hansestadt Hamburg, Germany; Mr Graf of the Tiefbauamt des Kantons Zürich Switzerland; Jacob Oertli of Swiss Federal Railways, Bern, Switzerland; Mr Cereda of Autostrade 1° Tronco, Milano and Mr Natali and Mr Ricci, Autostrade 2° Tronco, Genoa, Italy.

Furthermore, we would like to thank the many individuals and their companies who have helped us, including: David McKittrick of EC Environmental Systems, England; Maurice Green of Van Campen, the Netherlands; Thomas Ottmer of MICE, Belgium; Eric Plinius of Akustic & Lyd Plinius & Co, Copenhagen, Denmark; Mr Brero, IPSE, Turin, Italy; Mr Veldhoen of Veldhoen Raalte, Raalte, the Netherlands; Victor Groenewegen of Van Lee, the Netherlands, and Derek Rogers of Lighting and Acoustic Design. We would also like to thank those manufacturers, suppliers and installers of barriers who have supplied information about their products and services.

Locations of photographs

Introduction

Background

The growth in the use of noise barriers across Europe, the USA, Australia and the Far East reflects the growing concern of the general public about noise pollution caused by major infrastructure projects, in particular roads and railways. This concern about the adverse effects of noise in the environment has, in turn, led governments to create the legislative framework that has motivated the responsible authorities to mitigate noise in urban, semirural and even rural localities.

The growing demand for a quieter environment has caused the noise barrier market to grow considerably across Europe in recent years. This, no doubt, will continue to grow across continental Europe and also in the UK, as project designers respond to increasing environmental concerns and have to comply with improved noise attenuation guidelines, and more demanding legislation. The acoustic and aesthetic standards of barriers have improved considerably and will continue to improve at an accelerated rate as information and expertise is disseminated across borders. These pressures for change will be given added impetus as European design standards are being developed and international working groups such as the Organisation for Economic Co-operation and Development (OECD) research the problem of solving transport noise problems.

It is often tempting to regard traffic noise as a twentieth century phenomenon, but nothing could be further from the truth. The Romans were all too familiar with the unwanted noise of wheels on stone streets and issued a decree which banned the use of chariots on the streets of Rome at night. Sadly for the Romans, their leaders did not have a monopoly of acoustic wisdom: Julius Caesar passed a law which required all goods deliveries in Rome to be made at night. Not content with creating this noise nuisance, Claudius subsequently extended the law to all towns in Italy and Marcus Aurelias imposed it on every town in the Roman Empire.

The fall of the Roman Empire heralded an apparent decline in interest in controlling the adverse effects of traffic noise. There appears to be little reference to the problem for many centuries until the invention of the internal combustion engine irrevocably changed the aural landscape. It took only three decades of motor transport to convince the British Government to introduce legislation to control the noise emitted by motor vehicles. A simple act, passed in 1929, predated the invention of any means of measuring noise: it relied on a policeman's and then the court's judgement to decide if the offending vehicle was too noisy.[1]

Traffic noise barriers have been installed in the UK since the 1960s. Major road schemes across the country have typically utilised earth mounds and timber fences to mitigate noise and visual intrusion: in certain locations, however, these natural-looking barriers are visually out of place. There is a need to design such barriers, now termed 'environmental barriers', in appropriate, forward looking and environmentally conscious ways.

There is a particular need for this change in attitude to design in the UK, where noise barrier design is still in its infancy when compared with both the achievements and plans in many other countries. There are many different reasons why the development of noise barriers in the UK has been less ambitious and extensive than in other European countries. Four of the main reasons are:

- the effects of the Land Compensation Act, 1973;[2]
- the different targets for community noise levels set by each country;
- the official traffic noise calculation procedure tends to overestimate barrier performance;
- the lack of a programme to reduce noise on existing roads in the UK.

The Land Compensation Act was introduced to provide compensation to owners of property which was devalued as a consequence of public works, irrespective of whether the property or part of the property was needed for the execution of those works. Under the Act, regulations were introduced in 1975, which enabled part of the compensation for householders to be the provision of noise insulation.[3] This is available where the exposure to noise is increased to 68 $dBL_{A10,18hr}$ due to a new or altered road, and where certain other criteria are met. The noise level is the arithmetic average of the A-weighted sound pressure levels exceeded for 10 per cent of each of the hours between 0600 and 2400 hours.

Throughout the time that the Land Compensation Act has been on the statute book, it has been the policy of the UK Government to provide screening in preference to noise insulation. All too often the cost of barriers was balanced against the cost of noise insulation and this simple fiscal test resulted in insulation being offered to owners of affected properties. It is worth noting, however, that a preference for screening was reaffirmed by the Government as recently as 1994 in its planning guidance on noise given in *PPG 24* in 1994.[4]

The Land Compensation Act was an enlightened piece of legislation and there is much to commend in it. However, it is an unfortunate consequence of the subsequent Noise Insulation Regulations that the qualification threshold noise level has become a *de facto* design target level in the absence of any other official guidance. In contrast, many other European countries have introduced legislation on design targets which are often significantly lower than the 68 $\text{dB}L_{A10,18hr}$ level used in the UK. Notable amongst these are the Netherlands and Denmark, where the permitted level is 55 $\text{dB}L_{Aeq,12hr}$ (a notional steady A-weighted sound pressure level of equal energy to the time varying noise over a 12 hour period, usually between 0800 and 2000 hours), a target which results in environmental noise which is, subjectively, only half as loud as the level permitted in the UK. Where target levels are lower, it follows that screening will be more robust and substantial. It also means that in those countries the use of screening is more widespread and that greater experience has been gained in the design, manufacture and construction of noise barriers.

In the UK, calculations of road traffic noise levels are made following the Department of Transport's method.[5] This models traffic as a single line source for all roads, except those dual carriageways where the central reserve is unusually wide or the carriageways are at different heights. The single noise source is located 3.5 m in from the nearside edge of the carriageway, which is a fair approximation for single and narrower dual carriageway roads. Where barriers are used, this model effectively places all of the traffic close to the barrier, where it will receive the maximum benefit from the barrier. Studies have shown that this can lead to an overestimate of barrier performance of over 2 dB for wide dual carriageway roads.[6]

Another reason for the absence of substantial barriers in the UK is the lack of a policy to reduce noise exposure from existing roads. Such policies, often known as 'black spot' policies, are common in the rest of Europe; many countries often spend as much on quietening existing roads as on the control of noise from new schemes. Historically, the official reason for not adopting a black spot policy in the UK has been that owners of properties along these noisy roads would have been compensated at the time of the construction and, therefore, it would be offering double compensation to also provide screening. A few exceptions have been made where particularly noisy roads were constructed prior to the introduction of the Land Compensation Act, but this does not help those people affected by noise from roads where the traffic growth has been much greater than forecast. Nor, it seems, can these people expect an early change in their situation, as the new Government elected in 1997 confirmed its opposition to the quietening of existing roads within months of being elected.[7]

New major roads are generally planned to avoid residential areas and, therefore, the communities exposed to the highest levels of traffic noise are often found along established, heavily trafficked roads within cities and other developed areas. In these situations housing is often very close to the road and reducing noise would require the use of tall barriers. In such locations, timber fencing, which is the most frequently used system in the UK, is often visually inappropriate. This problem has been recognised by the authorities in those countries which try to control noise in these areas, and thus a range of more suitable materials and barrier forms has been explored and developed.

In one respect, the long-standing reluctance to tackle the relentless increase in traffic noise in the UK has had some benefit. During this period a vast range of barrier types has been used and tested abroad. Planners in the UK now have a good idea of what can be achieved, in terms of acoustic mitigation, visual aesthetics of the barriers, and the effect these, often large scale, constructions can have in different environments. It has also given designers and the responsible authorities, as well as local people, a chance to become accustomed to seeing these elements in the environment. There is now a real public demand for the provision of well designed and appropriate structures in the landscape.

Environmental noise barrier terminology

One of the primary objectives of this publication is to encourage a universal and appropriate use of terminology for describing noise barriers which are variously called noise fences and screens, or acoustic barriers and, more recently, environmental barriers.

The lack of an agreed terminology led to considerable deliberation over the title for this book as the current use of terminology in this field can often be misleading. For example, the term 'environmental barrier', signifies a noise or visual barrier to the Highways Agency and its agents in the UK, but in some countries it may well mean some kind of geotextile barrier that isolates contaminated soil. Other professions may also use the term differently; ecologists may use it to describe fencing that could protect wildlife such as deer, badgers or newts from entering a road corridor.

It also appears that the terms used to describe barriers could disguise their purpose, thus confusing designers and clients alike, and this makes it more difficult for the public to understand the objectives and intentions of the proposals. This situation helps to create a climate of misunderstanding and a lack of clarity of purpose. At worst, it causes lack of trust between the developer and the public. It is, therefore, extremely important to categorise these barriers/screens/fences according to their function to make sure that everyone understands their purpose.

Generally, the Highways Agency categorises noise barriers and landscape or visual barriers by the generic term 'environmental barriers'. This term encompasses all barrier/fence/screen/mound types, regardless of whether their function is to mitigate noise or to protect views and/or the landscape. It should be stressed that environmental barriers in the UK are thus designed to reduce noise and to protect views in the landscape.

To avoid further confusion, it is also important at the outset to use the appropriate aural terminology in describing a barrier, for they are often called acoustic barriers or sound walls as well as noise barriers. Since it is common to define noise as unwanted sound, it seems appropriate, therefore, to use the term 'noise barriers' as their function is to attenuate a specific traffic noise problem. Thus, the general term 'environmental noise barrier' may be used to encompass every type of structure used to reduce noise.

Alternatively, where a barrier is designed to mitigate certain unwanted views, or to screen a disturbing alteration or addition to the landscape, it may best be termed a 'visual barrier'. It is often the case that the barrier is intended to mitigate both noise and views, because where there is a noise problem there is usually a visual problem as well. In this case it should be termed a 'noise/visual barrier'. This, however, is not as simple as it may seem, for it is also important to recognise that, although a barrier may have a dual function, very often the heights necessary for each function and the type of barrier required may need to be different.

A certainty of function is especially important when considering materials, because these may have an effect on the height of the barrier. Due consideration must be given to its horizontal alignment and its appearance, because the barrier will be subject to close scrutiny throughout the design and planning processes. Without this clarity of function, the issues are clouded and this may result in the design of an inappropriate barrier.

There is also some confusion as to whether a barrier should be called a fence or a screen or perhaps just a barrier, as is evidenced by the current use of the terms noise fence, noise screen and noise barrier. Although, in many cases, it may be possible to call a barrier a screen or a fence, in some cases this is inappropriate because it suggests a much less substantial structure than would be needed to control noise adequately.

Noise is a landscape issue

Although the emphasis of this book is on noise and noise barriers, noise is also a landscape issue,[8] in that it has a great impact on the perception of the character and quality of the landscape. A landscape assessment may describe the character of a landscape as having a quiet or tranquil setting, or as being noisy. This affects the categorisation of the landscape quality of an area, which may deteriorate with the presence of noise. Whereas some people may concentrate on the negative impact that barriers have on the landscape due to their scale, appearance or other perceived undesirable qualities, the noise itself may well have an adverse effect on people's enjoyment of the landscape and can have, therefore, an adverse effect on landscape quality, land scape character and the quality of life. The experience of sitting in a garden, listening to bird song, is quite different from and more pleasant than sitting in a garden which is dominated by the roar of traffic noise. In rural environments too, enjoyment of the landscape and leisure activities may be diminished by the presence of noise. More often than not, noise is the first and only indicator of the presence of development or infrastructure projects, as these schemes are often well screened by planting.

Although the reduction of noise in a given location through the use of barriers could help to improve the problem that a development has caused to the environment, it may create others. It is important to acknowledge the effect these often large and imposing barriers may have on other environmental issues. They may affect views, light, microclimate, access, wildlife and birds. These structures, which may be 5–10 m high, or even in exceptional circumstances up to 20 m, should be integrated, as far as possible, into the

1.1 Twenty metre high barrier protecting residential blocks on the Périphérique, Paris

local surroundings and all environmental issues relating to them be properly examined (Figure 1.1). A barrier should reduce noise to the required levels, and be acceptable to the planning authorities but, to be truly successful, it must merit approval from local inhabitants. In order to satisfy these conditions, the barrier must be designed to integrate well into its surroundings. When the wrong type of barrier is constructed, which degrades landscape character and diminishes landscape quality, it will inspire local animosity. Social surveys have shown that where this is allowed to happen the public's perception of any acoustic benefit is noticeably reduced. An extreme example of the problems caused by failing to consult local people occurred in Oregon where the highways authority was forced to remove a noise barrier because of local hostility.[9]

Landscape architects prefer not to see noise or visual barriers, as they may have a significant impact on the landscape. Where the need for barriers outweighs the sum of the other negative environmental effects, it is the task of the landscape architect to help to improve the visual environment for those living adjacent to intrusive developments, and to maintain the integrity of the landscape. Aesthetic and visual integration is not a simple task, not least because in many cases there is likely to be opposition to barriers due to their scale and appearance. However, it is possible to satisfactorily integrate these structures into the landscape with sensitive design solutions: employing appropriate vertical and horizontal alignments; with sympathetic use of materials and combinations of materials; with creative and appropriate use of pattern, colour and texture; and especially with imaginative planting. When designed well, environmental noise barriers and visual barriers may be satisfactorily integrated into the landscape and be acceptable to local people.

It must also be remembered that environmental concerns are growing and that people no longer accept mediocre standards and poor quality service.

The importance of protecting the integrity of the countryside and people's enjoyment of it should not be underestimated. If new infrastructure is required, the necessary measures must be taken to lessen or negate potential negative impacts and this should be undertaken as an integral part of the work. Mitigation must be seen as an essential part of any scheme. In terms of landscape architecture, it forms a major part of the landscape objectives, strategy and design.

Barrier design is a complicated process. The best results are likely to be achieved through the co-ordinated services of qualified acousticians, civil and structural engineers, landscape architects and architects. Other professional expertise may also be required, including advice from geotechnical, ecological, irrigation, horticultural and other environmental and planning specialists.

It appears that the environmental thinking and practice relating to environmental noise control is less advanced in the UK than in many other parts of Europe. There are, however, signs that the British public is no longer prepared to accept the provision of inadequate environmental solutions. Continental European scale barriers have been installed at a few sites in the UK and a wider range of barrier materials can now be seen alongside roads, particularly on the busier motorways in southern England. The process of improvement of standards and provision is likely to receive a boost through the harmonisation of European standards, as consultation procedures have already begun. It is proposed to set the same noise control objectives for all European Union countries and also to map the existing levels of environmental noise throughout the European Union. If implemented, this should mark a welcome shift in emphasis away from compensation in favour of better provision of noise mitigation.

Barrier use: a contrast in provision

It makes good sense to include local residents and authorities in the planning of barriers at the earliest stage possible, as is the case in the Netherlands or Denmark, for example. This is beneficial in terms of cost and the smooth running of the project. It also avoids misunderstanding if planners work within a framework of trust and consultation. At present in the UK the public is included in this process at too late a stage and consequently feels marginalised and helpless. A major sea-change is needed to ensure that local people are involved in this process early enough. Of course, the design process should not be annexed by the public, nor should barriers be designed by a committee of lay people; nevertheless, people affected by new or extended traffic systems should feel that they have a say in the solutions and should be kept fully informed about developments.

When considering the problems of noise and visual intrusion, it is also important to look at alternative methods of mitigation other than through the use of barriers, including the use of quiet road surfaces, the insulation of properties or even tunnelling. For the reduction of noise, all these options need to be considered individually and in conjunction with one another, as

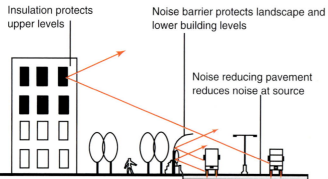

Insulation protects upper levels

Noise barrier protects landscape and lower building levels

Noise reducing pavement reduces noise at source

1.2 Composite noise reduction

1.3 Core samples of running surfaces. Left to right: twin layers of porous asphalt with rubber coating, single layer of porous asphalt with rubber coating, single layer porous asphalt, porous concrete, dense asphalt

the optimum noise and landscape mitigation strategy may involve using a number of solutions (Figure 1.2). In the Netherlands, for example, the extensive use of porous asphalt has significantly reduced road traffic noise (Figures 1.3 and 1.4). Reducing tyre/surface noise in this way allows designers and planners to keep barrier heights to a minimum. This, in turn, may minimise environmental effects and reduce the overall capital costs of a scheme. At present, over a third of Dutch motorways are surfaced in porous asphalt. It is the intention that, in time, the whole network will be treated similarly, as a response to an increase in the maximum speeds on motorways in Holland from 100 kph to 120 kph which increased noise levels by some 2 dB. The Dutch Noise Abatement Act states that 'measures should be taken to level down the increase of the noise level (stand still principle)'.[10]

1.4 Edge of porous asphalt running surface

1.5 Mature aluminium absorptive barrier, Hamburg

Compared with the UK, noise barriers in countries such as Germany, the Netherlands and France, form a greater part of the urban and semirural landscape and have done so for several decades. Absorptive barriers, namely barriers comprising materials that absorb noise, have been part of the German Autobahn system in and around cities for many years (Figure 1.5), whereas in the UK the construction of low, timber, sound-reflective fences has been the norm. In much of the rest of Europe care has been taken not only to provide barriers of the correct scale, but also to investigate the use of a wide range of materials and construction techniques. Of course, mistakes have been made and now many barriers appear dated and strangely out of place in the landscape. However, credit should be given to the planners responsible for their commitment to protecting people and the environment from unwanted noise and disturbing views.

Since the early days of noise barrier installation, great steps forward have also been taken in continental Europe with regard to noise reduction target levels, noise barrier design and appropriate consultation processes. In Denmark, for example, a select group of designers was recently set a challenge to design a new barrier for an improved road in inner-city Copenhagen. Five companies submitted plans and built sections of their proposed barrier *in situ*. The public was then asked to choose a preferred design. The winning design has since been chosen, and adapted for final construction (Figures 1.6–1.9).

Although environmental noise barrier construction could be regarded as a necessary evil, in continental Europe every effort is made to make a virtue out of necessity. Barriers are now part of the fabric of the environment, so designers, in consultation with environmental agencies and local residents, take great care to make them blend with their surroundings as well as ensuring that they provide effective noise mitigation. Although some barrier solutions are far from perfect and their construction raises questions about severance, personal safety and light, particularly in urban areas, the fact that they have been erected shows a practical commitment to public well-being

1.6 Competition entry 1996, Copenhagen

1.7 Competition entry 1996, Copenhagen

1.8 Competition entry 1996, Copenhagen

and the integrity of the environment. The case for environmental responsibility is gaining public support; environmental noise barriers should gain acceptance as people learn more about the issues at stake. Barriers may not be regarded as prestigious structures, but this does not mean that they should not be designed with care. They will be seen by millions of people every year and can have a significant effect on the public's aural and aesthetic appreciation of the landscape.

The landscape of the British Isles is like no other, particularly in terms of its intimate scale and varied character, so what is built elsewhere cannot simply be translocated. It has often been argued by planners in the UK that the scale of continental European barriers is often inappropriate to the smaller-scale landscapes of the British Isles. The argument that continental European solutions and designs cannot be adapted is now largely discredited,

1.9 Competition entry 1996, Copenhagen

based as it is on a lack of imagination, laziness and a reluctance to accept the scale of the problems presented by today's transport corridors. It is also an excuse for failing to allocate the appropriate budget for environmental protection. The difference in standards in the UK compared with elsewhere in Europe may suggest that the British people are less disturbed by noise pollution. No studies have revealed any differences in the effects of noise on the daily quality of life or health of all individuals of different nationalities, however. Indeed, the World Health Organisation has issued its own guidelines on acceptable environmental noise which are uniform throughout the world.[11] The OECD reported that traffic noise at typical levels of emission does not cause any immediate risk of hearing loss, but there are other important nonauditory negative effects.[12]

If the environment is to be improved for those people who are affected by transport noise, it is necessary to see and understand what can be achieved by studying the potentials of materials, and contemporary and past examples of what has been achieved elsewhere. Furthermore, continuing changes in attitude and legislation will be needed to ensure that a quieter, yet visually acceptable, environment is provided both in cities and in the countryside.

References

1. *The Motor Cars (Excessive Noise) Regulations, 1929, No. 416*, HMSO, London.
2. *Land Compensation Act (1973)*, HMSO, London.
3. Department of the Environment (1975) *Statutory Instruments, 1975, No. 1763 Building and Buildings. The Noise Insulation Regulations*, HMSO, London.
4. Department of the Environment (1994) *PPG24: Planning and Noise*, HMSO, London.
5. Department of Transport, Welsh Office (1988) *Calculation of Road Traffic Noise*, HMSO, London.
6. English, C.E. and Swift, C. (1993) Assessing Noise of Wide Motorways, *Proceedings of the Institute of Acoustics* **15**(4), 807–14.
7. Extract from Hansard (11 July 1997) reprinted in: *Acoustics Bulletin* **22**(4), 33.
8. English, C.E. and Kotzen, B. (1994) Integrating European Scale Barriers into the English Landscape, in Proceedings of a joint IHT/ENBA seminar: *Environmental Noise Barriers – A New Perspective*, 10 November 1994, Maidenhead, England.
9. The Transportation Research Board (1982) *Highway Noise Barriers*, National Academy of Sciences, Washington, DC, p. 11.
10. Padmos, C.J. (1995) Development of Low Noise Surfacing in the Netherlands, in *International Conference on Roadside Noise Abatement*, November 1995, Madrid.
11. World Health Organisation (1980) *Environmental Health Criteria 12: Noise*, WHO, Geneva.
12. Organisation for Economic Co-operation and Development (1995) *Roadside Noise Abatement*, OECD, Paris, p. 20.

Defining the need for barriers 2

Legislation and policy

Introduction

The provision of a traffic noise barrier on any road depends on both the relevant legislation and on the adopted policies of the highways authority concerned. In general, the design and construction of all public roads in the UK must comply with the legislation extant at the time of granting of orders for its construction, but policy regarding the provision of traffic noise barriers varies according to which authority is responsible for the road.

The current legislation in the UK concentrates primarily on providing a framework for compensating those adversely affected by road traffic noise. Government policy, however, is increasingly addressing the need to reduce traffic noise at source.

Since the 1970s, legislation and policy have concentrated on mitigating the effects of new schemes, and it is not surprising, therefore, that it has dealt exclusively with the effects of road traffic noise. The 1990s have, due to a combination of environmental and economic pressures, seen a revival in the building of railways in the UK. Potentially this could have led to inequitable situations, where those communities affected by new railway noise were disadvantaged when compared with those affected by new road noise. The Government's response was to introduce new regulations designed to treat those affected by train noise in an identical manner to those affected by road traffic noise. Initially this approach seems entirely reasonable, but implicit in it is the presumption that the current policy with respect to road traffic noise is appropriate for the late twentieth century and beyond. At a time when it is becoming increasingly clear that road traffic noise abatement in the UK is falling considerably short of the standards being achieved in many other countries, many saw this as a lost opportunity to improve the standards of provision.

The Land Compensation Act, 1973

The Land Compensation Act, 1973[1] was introduced to provide a mechanism to compensate those who were adversely affected by the execution or operation of public works. This, of course, included all road schemes and the Act has been pivotal in shaping the country's response to the problem of traffic noise. This Act made provision for homeowners to be offered noise insulation provided that certain qualification criteria were met. It also allowed for payments to be made where residential properties suffered a drop in value due to the adverse effects of a road scheme, including noise.

The Noise Insulation Regulations, 1975

The Noise Insulation Regulations (amended 1988)[2, 3] set out the qualification criteria that apply in England and Wales for determining those residential properties which may be offered noise insulation under the Land Compensation Act. Grants are only available for residential buildings within 300 m of the edge of the carriageway under construction or being altered. To qualify for a grant, properties affected by noise from a new road or carriageway must meet all three of the following tests:

- the total expected maximum traffic noise level within 15 years of opening of the road scheme, i.e. the relevant noise level, must not be less than the specified noise level (defined as 68 dB$L_{A10,18hr}$);
- the relevant noise level shall be at least 1 dB(A) more than the prevailing noise level, i.e. the total traffic noise level obtaining prior to the start of work to construct or improve the road;
- the contribution to the increase in the relevant noise level from the new or altered road must be at least 1 dB(A).

The regulations place a duty on the highway authority to offer grants, or to carry out noise insulation works, where the above conditions are met. However, separate provisions are made for properties affected by highway alterations that do not include the provision of new carriageways. In these cases, there is a discretionary power to provide noise insulation grants provided that, as a minimum requirement, the same three qualification tests are met. The discretionary nature of this power, with no clear guidance on when it should be exercised, inevitably leads to anomalies in its application. Many highways authorities adopt more stringent standards and require that there is a 3 dB increase in the relevant noise level above the prevailing noise level, whereas others have required a 5 dB increase. However, for many motorway widening schemes, the Highways Agency has adopted the same criteria as used for new roads.

The regulations also enable noise insulation to be provided for dwellings which are seriously affected by road construction noise for a substantial period of time. This again is a discretionary power and there are no published definitions of 'seriously affected' or 'substantial period', which can lead to discrepancies in application.

The equivalent regulations adopted in Scotland,[4] and more recently in Northern Ireland,[5] differ from those described above in their treatment of the relevant noise level. Rather than forecasting the noisiest year within 15 years of opening, the highways authority is required to review the traffic noise from the road regularly and update the insulation accordingly. This has the advantage of subsequently insulating further properties affected by increased noise from roads that are subject to greater traffic flows than forecast prior to the opening of the road.

At the present time there are only powers to provide noise insulation for residential buildings, although the Government has been considering the extension of these powers to include hospitals and schools.[6] Another aspect of the regulations that urgently requires modification is the 300 m limit for eligibility. When this was first introduced it reflected the fact that traffic conditions could not possibly cause the qualification threshold to be exceeded outside the area covered by this limit. Today's greater traffic flows and speeds now mean that properties considerably outside the 300 m distance limit could meet the noise criteria for insulation, but there is no mechanism which can be used to offer this to the affected properties.

The Highways Act, 1980

It has always been recognised that control of noise at source is more desirable than providing noise insulation at the affected properties. As traffic volumes and noise levels increase, the numbers of properties adversely affected grow and it becomes an increasingly viable option to provide screening for roads. Clause 246 of the Highways Act[7] gives highways authorities the powers to acquire land to mitigate the effects of a new or altered road. The purchase of such land must commence prior to the opening of the road scheme.

Clause 282 of the Act gives powers to a highways authority to provide or improve the traffic noise barriers on its own land at any time. There are no powers to acquire, by compulsory purchase, land for screening after the scheme is completed; however, this can be done with the agreement of the owner of the adjacent land.

National Government policy

The responsibility for the motorway and trunk road system rests with the Department of Transport (DoT) and, therefore, Government policy is directly applicable to these roads. In 1990, the Government summarised its policy on reducing road traffic noise in the White Paper, *This Common Inheritance*.[8] This stated that the lines and levels for roads were selected to minimise noise and that noise barriers and mounds were used to reduce noise. It also anticipated that quieter road surfaces would be used to reduce noise at source.

In 1992 the DoT permitted the use of porous asphalt in urban and noise sensitive locations. At the same time it banned the use of concrete running surfaces for roads carrying over 75 000 vehicles per day.[9] Earlier that year the DoT approved the use of exposed aggregate concrete, or whisper concrete.[10]

The effect of these decisions is to allow the use of surfaces such as porous asphalt, which is 3–4 dB quieter than hot rolled asphalt, and also whisper concrete, which is about 1 dB quieter than hot rolled asphalt, while banning the noisiest (concrete) surface.

The reductions in noise that can be provided by inherently quiet road surfaces are relatively modest when compared with what can be achieved with screening. As noted above, the increasing volumes of traffic and the concomitant increase in properties affected by noise has resulted in the more frequent use of noise barriers to control noise. There is no comprehensive policy for deciding when and where to use barriers. Instead, it is left to each project design team to decide where the use of barriers is justified. The DoT has issued guidance on the use of noise barriers in the *Design Manual for Roads and Bridges (DMRB)*[11] but, notwithstanding this, the *ad hoc* approach has led to a wide range of design standards being adopted. Often the objective is to ensure that noise levels are limited to just below the noise insulation qualification threshold; the results of this have often, and rightly, been described as maximising the noise nuisance. Some schemes use barriers to substantially improve the noise climate for nearby residents, whereas others use them merely to maintain noise levels at those obtaining prior to an improvement being implemented.

It is somewhat surprising that, among road designers, there remains a very cautious approach to the use of barriers, as the advice in *DMRB* is so very positive. In particular, the advice given on motorway widening is very strong and among the design objectives it lists:[12]

- all realistic opportunities for environmental improvement should be undertaken;
- all opportunities to enhance mitigation and provide new mitigation should be undertaken.

When discussing barriers, it lists as key issues:

- environmental barriers should make full use of current techniques and materials and be designed to solve site-specific problems;
- widening can be an opportunity to install better environmental barriers than those presently in place and to improve the quality of life for people living close to the motorway, even though traffic may be moved nearer to them.

A possible reason for at least some of the reluctance to follow the *DMRB* guidance is that all calculations of traffic noise, for environmental assessments and noise insulation purposes, must be carried out using the *Calculation of Road Traffic Noise (CRTN)* procedure.[13] This method deals with the performance of conventional reflective barriers, but has not been extended to include procedures for assessing absorptive barriers and the range of novel edge details which is now available. Clearly there is a need to update *CRTN* in order to give due credit for the additional expense of including these features in a road scheme.

Local government policy

Roads other than motorways and trunk roads are the responsibility of the County Councils and Unitary Authorities and, although these generally follow Government policy, they are free to adopt different policies. The use of traffic noise barriers provides a good example of the difference in approach used by the Highways Agency and local highways authorities. The practice of the Highways Agency is to consider their use where they are considered to be cost effective, which usually means that they are used to reduce noise levels to below 68 $dBL_{A10,18hr}$, thus avoiding the cost of noise insulation. Increasingly the cost of compensation claims under Part 1 of the Land Compensation Act has also been included in this analysis. Many local authorities go further than this and consider their use for properties exposed to lower levels of traffic noise. For example, in a recent survey of policy,[14] a quarter of these councils stated that they considered using barriers where properties would be exposed to more than 60 $dBL_{A10,18hr}$, and a further 13 per cent considered their use at a level of 65 $dBL_{A10,18hr}$. Some 16 per cent of councils also used criteria based on relative, rather than absolute, levels, with most of these considering the use of barriers where the traffic noise (L_{A10}) exceeded the background noise (L_{A90}) by 10 dB.

The use of the 'cost effective' test by national government leads to barriers being used predominantly to protect only relatively large residential areas. In contrast, over 40 per cent of local authorities will consider their use for isolated properties and over half would screen public open space and recreation areas. Schools and hospitals would be screened by 8 per cent of local authorities but, as these do not qualify for noise insulation or financial compensation under current legislation, they are unlikely to be treated at a national level.

Another example of the different approach taken by central and local government is in the treatment of existing noisy roads. Central government has no policy to provide mitigation on existing roads that have become noisy, unless a road alteration scheme is undertaken. At least two local authorities have, however, installed noise barriers alongside both their own roads and those under central government control, in cases where noise has increased to unacceptable levels.[14]

Alternative European approaches

When travelling throughout Europe, it is noticeable that different countries have developed their own distinct approaches to the use of noise barriers and quiet road surfaces in order to control traffic noise. In northern European countries in particular, the use of noise barriers is much more extensive than in the UK and the scale of the barriers is generally much larger. Also of note is the extensive use of quiet road surfaces, particularly in the Netherlands.

The different approaches are a clear result of the different policies adopted by each country. The most significant of these is that noise limits, or at least objectives, are set out in legislation. Often these limits are set at low levels and limits of 55 dBL_{Aeq} are frequently imposed. In the UK there is no legally

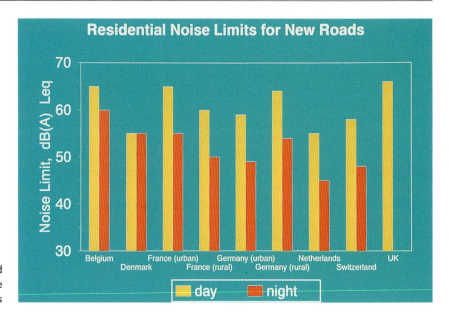

2.1 A comparison of road traffic noise limits in a sample of European countries

defined limit, although the 68 dB$L_{Aeq,18hr}$ noise insulation threshold has become a *de facto* limit. A review of European countries' standards revealed that the objectives which these countries set themselves lie in the range 55–65 dBL_{Aeq} for daytime noise exposure.[15] A sample of these countries' standards is given in Figure 2.1. It should be noted that all of the countries shown except the UK use the equivalent continuous noise level index to define their noise limits and, therefore, for ease of comparison, the UK's limit is converted to this index. That survey also revealed that many countries set night-time noise limits, whereas others simply rely on the use of a daytime limit. To a large extent the daytime limit will effectively limit night-time noise levels, because the night-time traffic volumes on most roads tend to be about 10 per cent of the total daytime flow. This assumption is not valid for those roads which have an unusually high flow of traffic at night, for example roads serving ports or food distribution depots, and increasingly the need for night-time noise limits is being addressed.

The enforcement of standards is vital if a better environment is to be realised. This is taken particularly seriously in the Netherlands and was demonstrated during the construction of the A28 motorway at Zeist. The motorway was built adjacent to a large housing development but its opening was delayed for 3 years until a suitable barrier was constructed. This delay was due to the failure to comply with noise regulations and mounting public concern about this omission. This barrier eventually took the form of an extremely large, visually successful, cantilevered concrete construction which extends over the hard shoulder of the east bound carriageway (Figures 2.2 and 2.3).

Another key difference is in the attitude towards noise from existing roads. Many countries have programmes for identifying the noisiest of their roads and implementing noise control measures. By dealing with the problem of existing roads, rather than treating just new and altered roads, far greater

2.2 Substantial concrete cantilevered barrier at Zeist, the Netherlands

2.3 Massive support structure on the public side of the barrier

numbers of people are benefiting from reduced noise levels. A striking example of this is found on the A16 at Dordrecht in the Netherlands. Here, traffic noise had increased over time and the local residents' association persuaded a member of parliament and an environment minister to sleep overnight in one of the apartments to assess the noise at first hand. The officials then understood how bad the situation was and subsequently a 10 m high cantilevered barrier of mixed materials was constructed (Figure 2.4).

Setting low noise levels as the design objective necessarily leads to larger and more extensive barriers being required. However, in those countries which set low noise limits, the use of quiet road surfaces and sound absorptive barriers does much to reduce the scale of barriers used to meet the objectives, and therefore produces more visually acceptable solutions.

The Noise Insulation (Railways and Other Guided Transport Systems) Regulations, 1996

The revival of the building of railways and tramways in the 1990s highlighted the anomaly that existed, whereby it was possible to provide noise insulation for those dwellings badly affected by road traffic noise but there was no means

2.4 Large cantilevered barrier protecting a housing area at Dordrecht, the Netherlands

of similarly treating properties affected by noise from these new rail systems. The Noise Insulation (Railways and Other Guided Transport Systems) Regulations, 1996[16] were introduced to meet this need, and were specifically designed to provide the same degree of protection as the existing regulations for road traffic noise. Again there is a duty to provide noise insulation for dwellings badly affected by noise from a new or additional railway line, and also a power to carry out similar works for properties affected by noise from altered existing rail systems. There are, however, some notable differences between the two sets of regulations.

First, train noise is measured using the equivalent continuous noise level index (dBL_{Aeq}), which acknowledges the intermittent nature of railway noise. Second, and more significantly, there are limits set for both daytime and night-time. There is a duty to carry out noise insulation works, or make a grant for such works, if all of the following conditions are met:

- the noise from a new or additional railway system exceeds a daytime noise level of 68 dB$L_{Aeq,18hr}$ or the night-time noise exceeds a level of 63 dB$L_{Aeq,6hr}$;
- the relevant noise level is at least a 1 dB(A) greater than the prevailing noise level;
- the noise from the railway makes an effective contribution to the relevant noise level of at least 1 dB(A).

The same minimum qualification criteria apply to the discretionary power to offer noise insulation for properties affected by noise from altered railways. The assessments are made following the calculation procedures set out in the *Calculation of Railway Noise*,[17] and in keeping with the procedures for road traffic noise, the relevant noise level is taken as the highest noise level expected to be created within 15 years of opening of the railway.

European Union directives

Throughout its life the European Union has sought to influence only those aspects of environmental noise which may be seen as possible obstructions on the path towards a single market. Thus its directives have been restricted to specifying maximum noise level limits for certain types of machinery, aeroplanes and road vehicles. However, in 1996 there was a notable departure from this policy with the publication of a Green Paper which addressed the need for a European noise abatement policy.[18] Significantly, the Green Paper notes that the previous policy of controlling and reducing road vehicle noise emission levels has not been successful in achieving a worthwhile reduction in environmental noise exposure.

The Green Paper reviews the noise impacts of eight major sources of environmental noise and identifies road traffic as the most important source, accounting for 90 per cent of the European Union exposure to daytime noise levels of more than 65 dBL_{Aeq}. Thus, some 80 million people in the European Union live in 'black areas' which are exposed to traffic noise at a level identified by the OECD as having a significant adverse effect on human health.[19] The OECD also defined 'grey areas' as being areas with daytime noise levels of 55–65 dBL_{Aeq} and the Green Paper notes that, although the number of people in black areas has been reduced, the number of people in grey areas has continued to rise. It is suggested that the EU adopts the following targets for the reduction of environmental noise exposure:

- phasing out of exposure above 65 dBL_{Aeq} (black areas);
- reducing the proportion of the population exposed to 55–65 dBL_{Aeq} (grey areas);
- noise levels in existing quiet areas should not rise above 55 dBL_{Aeq};
- exposure to more than 85 dBL_{Aeq} should never be allowed.

In order to achieve these objectives, it is proposed that there should be harmonisation of measurement and prediction methods and indices, improved information exchange and publication, a common environmental assessment framework, and an obligation on member states to take the necessary action to meet agreed minimum noise quality targets.

As a starting point the European Commission believes that noise exposure mapping should be carried out, either by survey or prediction, to identify both areas and populations exposed to excessive noise and the quiet areas to be preserved. The recommendations to reduce traffic noise concentrate on the reduction of noise generation rather than on controlling its spread. Practical noise reduction measures, such as the use of low-noise road surfaces and the reduction of road/tyre noise, are proposed, along with administrative controls including increased taxation, the introduction of more realistic vehicle noise tests, and the introduction of in-use noise testing of vehicles.

It is a matter of some regret that the UK's environment minister at the time of publication of the Green Paper greeted it with an emphatic rejection, claiming that political, cultural and lifestyle differences in member states underline the need to deal with these issues at a local level. The new Government has yet to comment on the proposals, but the European Commission is due to conclude its consultations in 1998 and, as the eventual decision will be made by qualified majority vote, no single government will be able to veto the decision.

Risk to health

It is beyond doubt that continued exposure to high levels of traffic noise has adverse effects on health. In 1980 the World Health Organisation (WHO) issued recommendations for the limitation of environmental noise.[20] It must be emphasised that, as its name implies, this organisation's work is solely related to health issues and, therefore, it follows that exposure to environmental noise at levels above its recommended limits must necessarily present a risk to health.

The WHO noted that exposure to daytime noise levels of 50 dBL_{Aeq} causes little or no serious annoyance in the community, and people may choose to live in areas with this level of noise exposure if other factors, such as the proximity of good schools, transport and employment, are present. It therefore recommended that 55 dBL_{Aeq} should be considered as a desirable environmental health goal for outdoor noise in residential areas. A night-time limit of 35 dBL_{Aeq} was set for intrusive noise within bedrooms, which approximates to an external level of 45 dBL_{Aeq}.

Performing tasks requiring concentration while exposed to high levels of traffic noise results in fatigue, annoyance and mistake making. Such effects are well understood by anyone who has worked in noisy conditions; however, the long-term effects on health are less well known. Several researchers have linked long-term exposure to traffic noise with increased risk of heart disease. Ising and Michalak[21] reported that increased stress caused by noise-induced communication disturbance results in changes in blood pressure, which in turn can lead to gastrointestinal disease, hypertension and other heart and circulatory diseases. Babisch and co-workers[22–24] studied the effects of exposure to traffic noise on large samples of men in various cities and reported an increased incidence of a range of heart diseases.

Design process

The realisation of any road or rail infrastructure project is a complex and iterative process. It will involve a wide range of specialists and, for a project to be successfully completed, all of the disciplines should act as an integrated team from the project's inception. It is always a false economy to design a project with a core team of mainstream engineers and then call in various environmental specialists to improve the chosen scheme. The results of that approach are invariably inadequate, with any mitigation that can be provided often looking like the afterthought that it clearly was.

Today, any major infrastructure project will require an environmental assessment to be made and an environmental statement to be published as part of the design process. Environmental assessment should also form part of the design process on smaller schemes for which the environmental assessment process is not mandatory. The Highways Agency has set out procedures for the environmental assessment of all of its projects in the DMRB (Volume 11).[25] This guidance requires that all aspects of the design of a road scheme should be considered throughout its planning stages, with increasing degrees of detail being required as the design develops. The process is designed to identify the effects of a scheme and to comment on their significance. Although considerable detail is given on how the effects should be quantified, no advice is given on the assessment of significance, and it has been left to individual scheme design teams to address the issue of the significance of individual effects and their cumulative effects. Official guidance on environmental assessment does not exist for non-Highways Agency road schemes nor for railways, and therefore the DMRB procedures are often adopted for these projects.

The nature of noise assessment is inherently different from that of the landscape assessment. The effects of noise can be quantified, whereas the landscape assessment has to be more subjective in its approach. Despite this difference, it soon becomes clear that the noise and landscape issues are, for many schemes, the most closely interrelated of all of the environmental design issues, because both deal exclusively with the effects of the scheme on people.

A difference between the two disciplines can be seen in their vocabularies. On many major schemes the landscape architect has been asked to assess the landscape mitigation as being 'essential' or 'desirable'. Such terms, however, have been used rarely by acousticians, which reveals the fact that their role has often been seen as the calculator of noise effects and benefits of mitigation measures, but not as a participant in the decision-making process. However, there is an increasing trend to openly define the environmental design objectives of a scheme and, therefore, all of the mitigation measures necessary to meet these objectives can rightly be described as essential. Thus, the terms 'essential' and 'desirable' are redundant.

Acoustic assessment

At the first stage of an environmental assessment the merits of several route options may need to be evaluated. For the initial assessment the *DMRB* advice is that numbers of noise-sensitive properties should be counted in a range of distance bands alongside each route. From this it may be concluded that it is desirable to site new routes away from existing development; however, this generally means introducing noise into a wide area which may otherwise be tranquil. It may often be better to select a route within an existing noisy corridor, such that the increases in noise would be small and controllable.

During the later stages of the assessment, the precise changes in noise level at all affected noise-sensitive properties must be evaluated. A calculation of the change in the percentage of the population that is likely to be bothered by noise must also be made. There is, however, no guidance given to the designer on what emphasis should be placed on the importance of these changes. Thus, to enable sensible development of noise mitigation proposals to be made, it is essential that clear objectives be set for the project. If these are not defined by the promoter of the scheme, it is the duty of the design team to propose and agree suitable targets. If this is not done, any noise mitigation that may be provided will be included on an *ad hoc* basis.

Different design objectives will be appropriate to different types of scheme; for example, a new road in a quiet greenfield site cannot reasonably be built without some increase in noise, but when widening an already noisy motorway it is quite feasible to design the scheme to reduce noise levels for local residents. It is not possible, therefore, for a single design objective to be set for all schemes, but it is desirable that similar objectives are set for schemes of a similar nature.

Objectives can be set in terms of absolute levels (levels not to exceed 68 dB$L_{A10,18h}$), relative levels (allow no more than 5 dB increase in noise), or in terms of the significance criteria set for the assessment of the scheme. The significance criteria are used as part of the final assessment of the scheme, but these must be known during the design stage in order that the relative importance of the various environmental effects of the scheme can be properly evaluated. Significance criteria are defined using descriptors such as minor, moderate and major to describe both the positive and negative effects of the scheme and may take account of the nature of the area affected by these changes. Thus, an increase in noise of, say, 10 dB may be described as moderately adverse if only a few isolated properties are affected, but would be seen as a major adverse effect if a large community was affected. If using significance criteria to set design objectives, it may be reasonable to avoid creating any effects worse than moderately adverse for a new road, whereas when dealing with alterations to existing roads the objective may be to provide at least minor beneficial effects.

Where projected noise levels exceed the design objectives, it will be necessary to evaluate all the noise-control options available. These include the use of low-noise road surfaces, lowering the road to utilise the screening of natural topography, the use of barriers and in some rare cases the use of speed restrictions. Often a combination of measures will be appropriate in order to meet both the acoustic requirements and the needs of other members of the design team. Arguably, any solution required to meet the design objectives can be described as essential, but this must be balanced against their impact on other issues, such as their visual impact, and due regard must be paid to the cost of the mitigation.

This latter point is seldom addressed properly. All too often a cost–benefit analysis is carried out which simply weighs the cost of the mitigation against the alternative cost of providing noise insulation and, increasingly, the cost of compensation for loss of property value. Such evaluations may be well-intentioned, but they are essentially flawed, because they place no value on the often considerable social and public health costs that increased noise exposure incur. This is particularly surprising because the hypothetical costs of delays caused to the travelling public are included in the cost–benefit analysis of a scheme, both when addressing congestion on existing roads and the likely delays that would be caused during the construction process.

In order that the noise effects of a scheme, with its proposed mitigation, can be balanced against the other issues, it is necessary to define the significance of any changes. These significance criteria must be developed as part of an overall assessment framework for the scheme and the descriptors must be consistent across all disciplines involved in the assessment. In general, the significance criteria should be similar for all projects, but they must also reflect local needs.

Landscape decision-making process

Landscape assessment

The Department of the Environment's *Planning Policy Guidance Note 13: Transport* (*PPG 13*), states that 'great care must be taken to minimise the impact of any new transport infrastucture projects, or improvements to existing infrastructure, on both the natural and built environment.' Furthermore, it states that 'new routes should make best use of the existing landscape contours and features to reduce noise and visual effects, having regard to safety and economic considerations. Additional screening through earth mounds or planting may be needed.'[26] This demonstrates the Government's commitment to protect and maintain the character and quality of any landscape and not just specially designated areas.

It is the landscape architect's role to try to minimise the effects of any scheme on the landscape. Where adverse effects occur, mitigation must be designed. Landscape objectives must be formulated to satisfy this national requirement. Local needs and issues also need to be considered.

The main landscape objective of a scheme should be to avoid any change in landscape character as this defines the nature of any particular location. Moreover, deterioration in landscape quality or visual intrusion must be avoided. Where a scheme is proposed in an already downgraded location, opportunities should be taken to improve these factors. The environmental assessment process requires that the significance of the effects of the scheme be identified. To do this, significance criteria are developed to reflect the local landscape conditions and take into account the scale of effects. Throughout the design process these criteria are used to evaluate and inform the design. The time factor is an important difference between landscape and most other environmental interventions: most large-scale mitigation will use immature plants which will only meet the design objectives once they have reached a reasonable state of maturity.

When dealing with landscape issues, the landscape architect has to use judgement to define and assess certain aesthetic qualities. This leads to comparatively subjective assessments and thus 'subjective' design and mitigation proposals, notwithstanding the fact that these may be based on the well-thought-out and rational principles of an experienced professional.

Assessment of visual intrusion

The assessment of visual intrusion must relate to people, as it is human beings who are affected by unsightly views. Visual intrusion relates directly to the distance of the viewer from the source of the visual disturbance. It must also relate to the magnitude of the visual disturbance and how this affects the quality of the view. Account must be taken of the number of people affected and their attitude towards the intrusion.

As part of the assessment and design process, visual intrusion and zones of visual influence plans (ZVI) are drawn up. These are used with the landscape character plans to help determine the type of barrier that would be appropriate. An example of where a barrier design meets these visual requirements is found in Bern, Switzerland. Here, a new viaduct crosses high above the River Aare. Most views of the viaduct are from the surrounding hillsides and the valley below. The strategic nature of the views has been acknowledged by varying the use of barrier materials relative to the visibility of the traffic on the viaduct. Where views of the traffic are less intrusive, a

2.5 Viaduct with transparent and opaque noise barriers

2.6 Transparent screen on a viaduct in zone of low visual intrusion

2.7 Opaque screen on a viaduct in a zone of high visual intrusion

barrier of transparent acrylic sheeting is employed, thereby maintaining the integrity of the form of the viaduct. However, where views of the traffic are deemed to be undesirable, the barrier is made from opaque perforated aluminium. An additional advantage of this solution is that the transparent sections also allow drivers views out from the road corridor (Figures 2.5–2.7). Visual intrusion will vary with time and plans must reflect this. A typical plan may show the changes in the magnitude of visual intrusion at three stages: the existing situation, the situation at the year of opening, and that 15 years on when the vegetation will have become established (Figure 2.8).

Another useful tool for determining the use of the correct forms, colours and textures is to produce colour, form and texture montages of the landscape within which the barrier is to be located. This allows the designer to decide whether to fit the barrier into its visual context or to try to make a more pronounced statement by contrasting forms, colours and textures.

Visual Intrusion Plan - Not to Scale

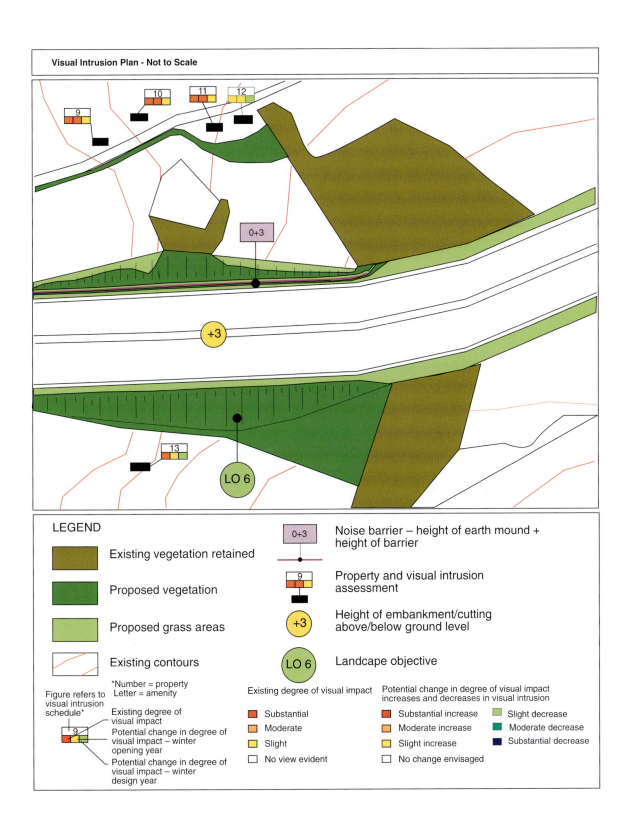

LEGEND

Existing vegetation retained

Proposed vegetation

Proposed grass areas

Existing contours

Figure refers to visual intrusion schedule*

*Number = property
Letter = amenity

Existing degree of visual impact

Potential change in degree of visual impact – winter opening year

Potential change in degree of visual impact – winter design year

0+3 — Noise barrier – height of earth mound + height of barrier

9 — Property and visual intrusion assessment

+3 — Height of embankment/cutting above/below ground level

LO 6 — Landcape objective

Existing degree of visual impact

- Substantial
- Moderate
- Slight
- No view evident

Potential change in degree of visual impact increases and decreases in visual intrusion

- Substantial increase
- Moderate increase
- Slight increase
- No change envisaged

- Slight decrease
- Moderate decrease
- Substantial decrease

2.8 Example of a visual intrusion plan

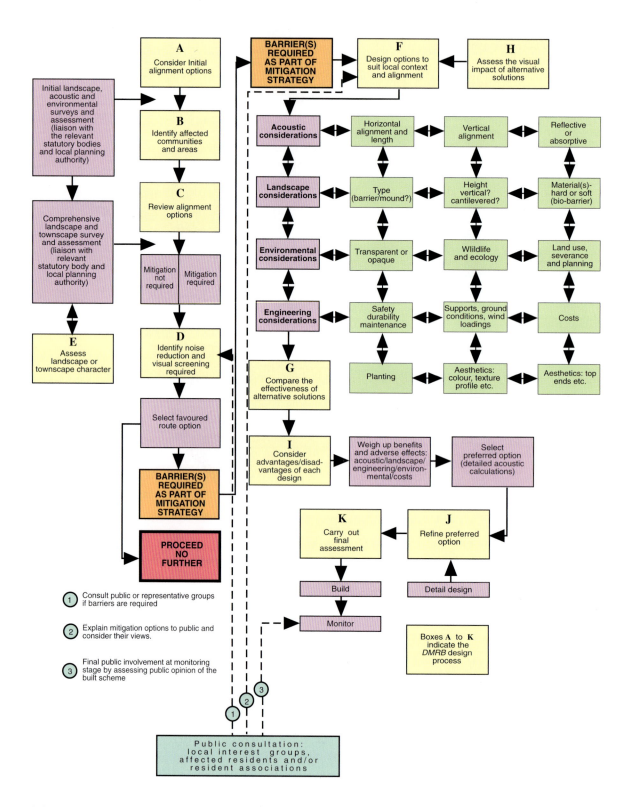

2.9 Mitigation and barrier selection process including stages of public involvement

DMRB assessment, consultation and design process

The Highways Agency sets out its design process in the *DMRB*, 'Stages in the Development of the Preferred Solution', under the heading the 'Environmental Barrier Design Process'.[27] The steps described to reach the preferred solution are laid out in a simplified form and in reality the process is more complex and iterative. The description of the procedure also does not mention the involvement of local government and other interest groups who are usually consulted at an early stage. Furthermore, the public who may be affected by the proposals are not mentioned, since they are consulted only after the preferred solution is announced.

The *DMRB* barrier design process is outlined below in stages A to K. Comments in braces amplify the process that takes place, indicate potential improvements that should be made, and notes where public involvement has been found to be beneficial in other countries. Figure 2.9 illustrates this procedure.

A. Consider initial alignment options

Investigate potential routes in order to minimise adverse environmental impact of the new road. {This includes initial acoustic, landscape and environmental surveys and assessments.}

B. Identify affected communities and areas

Highlight communities, facilities, recreation areas and designated areas alongside the route potentially affected by noise and visual intrusion. {This includes potential effects on landscape character and landscape quality.}

C. Review alignment options

Investigate modifications to vertical and horizontal alignments, in order to reduce the impact of the road in terms of noise and visual intrusion. {Stages A, B and C are an integrated process and may be repeated several times to accommodate the priorities of different disciplines and also incorporate the results of surveys as they become available. Local government would also be consulted.}

D. Identify noise reduction and visual screening objectives for each location

Determine location(s) and height(s) of barriers required to achieve the target reductions and establish the most effective profile providing an acceptable level of protection.

Confirm the need for a barrier before proceeding further. {Objectives should be set at the start of the process. If barriers are not required proceed no further. Although the locations and heights of barriers can now be defined for acoustic reasons, a knowledge of Stage E is required for the determination of landscape barriers. Consider other solutions including noise-absorptive pavements and insulation. If barriers are required, local interest groups and residents should be consulted.}

E. Assess landscape or townscape character

Identify the main features of the locality that could influence the range of barrier solutions considered, drawing on the landscape assessment for the route.

{Select the favoured route option}

{Stages A to E identify the possible routes and their mitigation. The least damaging route option is now chosen, paying due regard to cost.}

F. Design options to suit local context and alignment

Decide on the form of the barrier (earth mounding, fence, wall, structure or proprietary system, etc.) which would be most compatible with the neighbourhood. Select the most appropriate materials for the protected side compatible with the landscape or townscape character of the neighbourhood. {A barrier has two sides. Therefore also select the material for the traffic side of the barrier. An overall strategic design concept is also required which would provide an overall identity for the route. However, there may be conflicting objectives to be resolved between disciplines. Compromises may be required. The public should be informed about the possible mitigation options and their views should be considered.}

G. Compare the effectiveness of alternative solutions

Consider whether there is a case for using noise-absorbing or dispersing surfaces to reduce noise reflected from the barrier. Confirm whether the target reductions in noise would be acceptable. {Consideration of noise-absorptive and other mitigation types should have been considered at Stage D.}

H. Assess the visual impact of alternative solutions

Clarify the visual impact of alternative designs on affected residential or other sensitive areas using two- or three-dimensional sketches. Consider the use of planting to reduce the visual intrusion of the barrier itself. Consider the use of transparent materials to reduce adverse impacts such as loss of views or light. Confirm whether the target reductions in visual intrusion would be achieved. Should the barrier have the same appearance on the road-user side as that selected for the protected side? {All of the above should have been done at Stage F.}

I. Consider advantages/disadvantages for each design

Compare the characteristics of options, including implementation and maintenance costs, to inform choice of preferred option.

{Select the preferred option}

{The most appropriate solution for each barrier is now selected.}

J. Refine preferred option

At the detailed design stage refine the preferred solution to optimise visual and noise benefits.

Consider visual impact on the road user, including monotony – the need to provide drivers with visual relief as regards street furniture – harmonisation of lighting, signs, etc. {These latter issues should have been done at Stage F as they inform the choice of barrier. Barrier specifications should be written to ensure that the design objectives are fully realised.}

K. Carry out final assessment

Ensure all relevant criteria have been met.

{Build}

{Supervision should ensure that the design objectives are realised.}

{Monitor}

{The appropriate maintenance and monitoring should be carried out at appropriate intervals after construction to ensure that the barrier and other mitigation measures are performing adequately and that landscape measures develop as intended. The public should also be surveyed to assess their opinion of the scheme, to inform future designs.}

Summary of mitigation design strategies

In order to comply with the Government's guidance on the design of new transport infrastructure projects and improvements to existing infrastructure, a scheme must include the appropriate mitigation. This must be designed to minimise the impact of the scheme and, where this includes barriers, their impact must be minimised. Mitigation strategies will depend on the landscape character of the area and will vary for rural and urban locations. A summary of the ways to achieve this is given below, starting with the most effective (Figure 2.10).

Rural and semirural locations

1. Consider locating the route away from sensitive areas to avoid the need for barriers.
2. Where possible place the corridor in a tunnel where its effects are contained. (This may be deemed to be too expensive in most rural locations.)

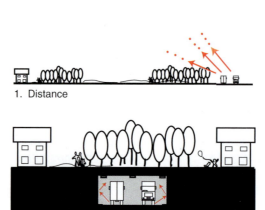

1. Distance

2. Tunnel/cut and cover

3. Cutting

4. False cuttings/earth mounds

5. Barriers – bio-barriers/vertical/cantilevered

6. Combined solution

7. Quiet surface (porous asphalt/whisper concrete)

(e.g. double glazing)

8. Insulation

2.10 Noise mitigation options

3. Contain the road within a cutting to provide acoustic and visual screening.
4. Should a barrier be required, select natural structures such as earth mounds with appropriate planting.
5. Where space is limited, consider bio-barriers to achieve a natural effect with planting on adjacent land if appropriate.
6. Vertical or cantilevered structures with planting on either side.
7. Where planting cannot be achieved the materials and detailing should be of a very high standard. If views need to be maintained then transparent barriers need to be considered.

Urban and developed locations

1. The corridor should be placed in a tunnel where its effects are contained. This can be cost effective in densely populated areas as the roof of the tunnel may be used for development or recreational purposes.
2. Contain the road within a retained cutting to minimise noise.
3. Apply noise-absorptive cladding to retaining walls.
4. Where barriers are required, close inspection should be made of the urban fabric, materials, historical and cultural context, colour and textural patterns to allow the barrier designed to tie into the local context. The location should be considered and a decision made as to whether to make the barrier an architectural feature or to blend it into the surroundings. In both cases planting can be used to advantage. Where appropriate, bio-barriers should be considered – they can used as urban hedges. In busy urban locations the materials and detailing should be of a very high standard. If views need to be maintained transparent barriers should be considered.

In both rural and urban locations, low-noise pavements should be considered at each stage as part of the solution. Noise insulation can be used in conjunction with a barrier to minimise its visual impact.

References

1. *Land Compensation Act, 1973*, HMSO, London.
2. Department of the Environment (1975) *Statutory Instruments, 1975 No. 1763, Building and Buildings. The Noise Insulation Regulations*, HMSO, London.
3. Department of the Environment (1988) *Statutory Instruments, 1988 No. 2000, Building and Buildings, The Noise Insulation (Amendment) Regulations*, HMSO, London.
4. The Scottish Office (1975) *Statutory Instruments, 1975 No. 460 (S.60), Building and Buildings, The Noise Insulation (Scotland) Regulations*, HMSO, London.
5. Department of the Environment for Northern Ireland (1995) *Statutory Rules of Northern Ireland, 1995 No. 409, Land, The Noise Insulation Regulations (Northern Ireland)*, HMSO, London.
6. *This Common Inheritance: Britain's Environmental Strategy* (1990) Cm 1200, HMSO, London, p. 212.

7. Department of Transport (1980) *The Highways Act, 1980*, HMSO, London.

8. *This Common Inheritance: Britain's Environmental Strategy* (1990) Cm 1200. HMSO, London, pp. 208–14.

9. The Department of Transport (1992) *Press Notice No. 204*, Department of Transport, London.

10. Highways Agency (1996) *Press Notice No. HA 168/96*, Highways Agency, London.

11. Highways Agency (1992) *Design Manual for Roads and Bridges*, Volume 10, Section 5, HMSO, London.

12. Highways Agency (1992) *Design Manual for Roads and Bridges*, Volume 10 Section 2, Part 1, HMSO, London.

13. Department of Transport, Welsh Office (1988) *Calculation of Road Traffic Noise*, HMSO, London.

14. English, C.E. (1997) Unpublished survey.

15. English, C.E. (1993) Strategies for Controlling Road Traffic Noise, in *Transport in the 90s*, Borough of Tower Hamlets, London.

16. Department of Transport (1995) *Statutory Instruments, No. 1996/428, Building and Buildings. Transport. The Noise Insulation (Railways and Other Guided Transport Systems) Regulations*, HMSO, London.

17. Department of Transport, Welsh Office (1995) *Calculation of Railway Noise*, HMSO, London.

18. European Commission (1990) *Green Paper on Future Noise Policy*, COM (96) 540 final, European Commission.

19. Organisation for Economic Co-operation and Development (1991) *Fighting Noise in the 1990s*, OECD, Paris.

20. World Health Organisation (1980) *Environmental Health Criteria, 12, Noise*, WHO, Geneva.

21. Ising, H. and Michalak, R. (1998) *Stress reactions due to noise-induced communication disturbance compared with direct vegetative noise effects*, personal communication.

22. Babisch, W., Ising, H., Gallacher, J. E. J., and Elwood, P. C. (1988) 'Traffic noise and cardiovascular risk. The Caerphilly study, first phase. Outdoor noise levels and risk factors', *Archives of Environmental Health*, **43**(6), 407–414.

23. Babisch, W., Ising, H., Kruppa, B. and Wiens, D. (1994) 'The incidence of myocardial infarction and its relation to road traffic noise – the Berlin case-control studies', *Environmental Health*, **20**(4), 469–474.

24. Babisch, W., Ising, H., Elwood, P. C., Sharp, D. S. and Bainton, D. (1994) *Archives of Environmental Health*, **48**(6), 406–413.

25. Highways Agency (1993) *Design Manual for Roads and Bridges*, Volume 11, HMSO, London.

26. Department of the Environment (1994) *Planning Policy Guidance Note PPG13: Transport*, HMSO, London.

27. Highways Agency (1994) *The Design Manual for Roads and Bridges*, Volume 10, Section 5, Part 1, HMSO, London.

Acoustic performance of barriers

3

Introduction

All too often noise barriers are built that provide little or no protection to the communities that they are intended to serve. There are others that, with a little more care in the design, could have provided significantly better screening than they achieve. To avoid these costly mistakes and to ensure that the greatest possible benefits are realised from every noise barrier, it is essential for designers to understand the basic principles of acoustic barrier theory.

Sound propagates from a source as a series of rapidly fluctuating pressure waves which expand spherically as they move away from the source (Figure 3.1(a)). These pressure waves create the sensation of noise when they reach the listener's ear. Although sound travels as waves it is often convenient to model sound propagation as straight lines or rays, which reach the listener or receiver either directly or indirectly after being reflected or diffracted by intervening surfaces (Figure 3.1(b)). The ray-tracing method is used below to describe commonly occurring screening scenarios.

Barrier theory

For an unscreened road, the most important sound transmission path is the ray travelling directly between the road and the receiver, known as the direct sound, $L_{p,dir}$. Another ray that will reach the receiver is the ray which strikes the ground and is reflected upwards to the receiver, $L_{p,grd}$ (Figure 3.2). There is a degree of destructive interference between these two rays which results in greater attenuation of the $L_{p,dir}$ than would be expected by geometrical spreading alone. The precise mechanism of this attenuation is not fully understood, but it is at its greatest where the propagation is over acoustically soft ground, such as grassland, and where the $L_{p,dir}$ is particularly close to the

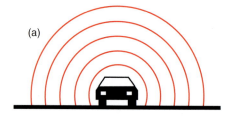
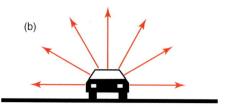

3.1 Sound propagation: (a) spherical spreading of sound; (b) ray model

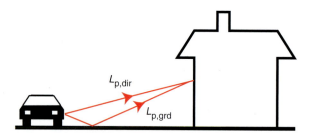

3.2 Unobstructed sound transmission paths

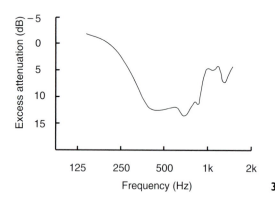

3.3 Excess attenuation for propagation over soft ground

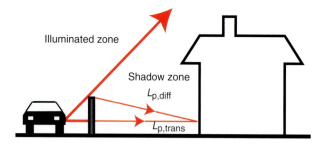

3.4 Key sound transmission for screened noise source

ground. This ground attenuation is frequency dependent and Hutchins *et al.*[1, 2] showed that the destructive interference predominantly occurs in a frequency range centred on 500 Hz (Figure 3.3).

The introduction of a barrier can greatly reduce the strength of the direct ray, although for most practical barriers this will remain a potential transmission path, $L_{p,\text{trans}}$. The important ray is now that diffracted downwards from the top edge of the barrier, $L_{p,diff}$ (Figure 3.4). The presence of the barrier also eliminates the $L_{p,grd}$ as a significant sound transmission path.

Considerable work has been carried out, using ray-tracing techniques, to establish the acoustic performance of a barrier, namely the difference between the $L_{p,dir}$ and the $L_{p,diff}$. Probably the most influential work is that of Maekawa[3] and this remains the basis of most of the practical methods for calculating barrier performance. Other workers developed the basic barrier theory and correlated the results with fieldwork.[4, 5] The theory developed calculates the acoustic performance of a vertical screen in terms of the Fresnel number N, which is defined as

$$N = 2\frac{\delta}{\lambda} \tag{1}$$

where δ is the path length difference (diffracted path length minus direct path length) and λ is the wavelength of sound in air. In the shadow zone, the area where the barrier breaks the line of sight between the source and the receiver, δ is defined as positive, and for rays propagating above the diffracting edge of the barrier, into the illuminated zone, δ is negative. Kurze and Anderson[5] gave the following equation for the insertion loss IL of a barrier:

$$IL = 5 + 20\log\frac{\sqrt{2\pi N}}{\tanh\sqrt{2\pi N}} \quad \text{(dB)} \quad \text{for } -0.2 < N < 12.5$$

$$= 24 \text{ (dB)} \quad \text{for } N > 12.5 \tag{2}$$

The above formula only applies to single vehicles at their closest point to the receiver and more complex expressions are available to describe the performance of a barrier for a stream of traffic. Fortunately for designers of barriers, they will seldom need to use these as the approved calculation methods for traffic noise provide the results in graphical or tabular form, and computer programs are usually available which implement these given methods. An understanding of the implications of the theory is necessary, however, if the optimum benefits are to be obtained from barriers.

First, from Equation (2) it can be seen that when a barrier just breaks the line of sight between the noise source and the receiver there is a 5 dB attenuation of noise, and there may be some reduction of noise for receivers in the illuminated zone. The barrier attenuation used in the UK's traffic noise calculation method[6] is shown in Figure 3.5. This gives a theoretical limit for barrier attenuation of about 20 dB(A) in the shadow zone; however, the required values of δ can seldom be realised and, in practice, a realistic limit is about 15 dB(A). The graph also shows that in the illuminated zone the barrier attenuation rapidly tends to zero at $\delta \leq -0.6$ and therefore there is little practical screening benefit to be gained in this region.

In the shadow zone, the difference in attenuation can be some 3 dB per octave for $\delta \geq 0.5\,\text{m}$ but, to avoid cumbersome, frequency-based computation, most calculation methods have adopted a composite value of N. These are derived from the known frequency spectrum of traffic and the

3.5 Potential barrier correction as a function of path difference

acoustic performance of a barrier, and typical composite N values correspond to the frequency range 300–500 Hz. Using a composite value of N allows the barrier calculations to be carried out in terms of A-weighted sound pressure levels (dB(A)).

From Equation (1) it can be seen that the acoustic performance of a barrier is frequency dependent. It should therefore be remembered that this, together with the loss of the mid-frequency ground attenuation, will always have the effect of biasing the received sound towards the low frequency end of the spectrum when a barrier is introduced.

Sound insulation

The attenuation achieved by a thin barrier can be compromised if it is not designed to ensure that the transmitted sound path does not significantly influence the overall noise level at the receiver. A contribution of 0.5 dB(A) to the overall level is commonly adopted as the limit for the contribution of the transmitted sound and this requires limiting the transmitted path as follows:

$$L_{p,trans} = L_{p,diff} + 10 \, \text{dB} \tag{3}$$

The sound insulation provided by a barrier is dependent upon many factors such as surface mass, stiffness, loss factors and the angle of incidence of the sound. The most significant of these is the surface mass of the barrier and many calculation methods adopt this as the sole descriptor of a barrier's sound insulation. In the UK the Department of Transport[7] gives the following formula for calculating the minimum required surface mass for a barrier:

$$M = 3 \times 10^{\left(\frac{A-10}{14}\right)} \, \text{kg/m}^2 \tag{4}$$

where A is the potential attenuation in dB(A) of the barrier ($L_{p,dir} - L_{p,diff}$).

sound, and consequently it is essential that any vegetative screen contains a high proportion of deciduous species.

There are some obvious drawbacks to using vegetative screens as the sole means of noise mitigation. Perhaps the main disadvantage if used for screening property is that the benefit is not immediate and it may take many years for the planting to develop, and in the meantime it may be necessary to provide other mitigation, such as noise insulation or a fence that may be allowed to deteriorate as the vegetation grows. By its very nature a tree belt is a constantly changing screen and in time may become more or less effective, and it is, therefore, not possible to precisely define the attenuation that will be provided. Thus, tree belts are not currently considered where accurate calculations have to be made for noise insulation assessments. A further consideration is that a degree of maintenance is required throughout the life of the screen if its optimum performance is to be achieved. There is evidence that the presence of vegetation on an earth mound provides a more effective screen than either the mound or the vegetation alone.[43] Consequently the role of vegetation is likely to be to either enhance the performance of earthworks, or to quieten open countryside where a precise reduction in noise is not required.

Acoustic performance testing

The European Committee for Standardization (CEN) has published a standard, EN 1793, which defines test procedures for measuring the acoustic performance of noise barriers and this has been adopted as a British Standard.[44-46] Part 1 of this standard gives a laboratory test method for measuring the sound absorption of a barrier, and Part 2 gives a laboratory test method for measuring the airborne sound insulation or transmission loss of a barrier. Both tests allow a single-number rating to be derived for the barrier and to calculate these it is necessary to use the standardised traffic noise frequency spectrum, which is given in Part 3 of the standard.

Laboratory testing does allow measurements to be made under controlled conditions, but there are certain drawbacks. The test sample is invariably perfectly installed in the test chamber in order to yield the optimum result, but this may not be representative of the performance achieved by a real installation. The test sample may be stiffer than the installed barrier as the panel elements will generally need to be cut to fit the test aperture, and also the top edge will be constrained within the aperture. The sound absorption test follows the procedure currently in use for the testing of other acoustic materials and allows the sample to be laid on the floor of the test chamber. This is acceptable for rigid, homogenous materials, but can yield misleading results for composite barrier systems.

To reduce the uncertainties introduced by laboratory testing, the CEN working group is developing an *in situ* test procedure for barriers using sound intensity techniques. This will allow both the sound absorption and the airborne sound insulation of barriers to be tested on site, and also provides a means of checking that the desired acoustic performance of a barrier is maintained throughout its life. Furthermore, it will allow the acoustic performance of bio-barriers to be quantified, because it is not practical to test these in a laboratory. The research for this is still at an early stage and it is not expected that the standard will be published for several years.

References

1. Hutchins, D. A., Jones, H. W. and Russell, L. T. (1984) 'Model studies of barrier performance in the presence of ground surfaces, Part 1 – Thin perfectly reflecting barriers'. *Journal of the Acoustical Society of America*, **75**(6), 1807–16.
2. Hutchins, D. A., Jones, H. W. and Russell, L. T. (1984) 'Model studies of barrier performance in the presence of ground surfaces, Part 2 – Different shapes'. *Journal of the Acoustical Society of America*, **75**(6), 1817–26.
3. Maekawa, Z. (1968) 'Noise reduction by screens', *Journal of Applied Acoustics* **1**, 157–73.
4. Rathe, E. J. (1969) 'Note on two common problems of sound attenuation', *Journal of Sound and Vibration*, **10**(3), 472–9.
5. Kurze, U. J. and Anderson, G. S. (1971) 'Sound attenuation by barriers', *Applied Acoustics*, **4**, 35–53.
6. Department of Transport and Welsh Office (1988) *Calculation of Road Traffic Noise*, HMSO, London.
7. Department of Transport (1976) *Noise Barriers – Standards and Materials*, Technical Memorandum H14/76, Department of Transport, London.
8. Hothersall, D. C., Chandler-Wilde, S. N. and Crombie, D. H. (1993) Modelling the performance of road traffic barriers, in Proceedings of TRL meeting, *Traffic Noise Barriers*, pp. 22–37.
9. Watts, G. R. (1995) 'Acoustical performance of parallel Traffic Noise Barriers', *Applied Acoustics*, **47**, 95–119.
10. Tobutt, D. C. and Nelson, P. M. (1990) *A Model to Calculate Traffic Noise Levels from Complex Highway Cross-sections*, Report RR 245, Transport and Road Research Laboratory, Crowthorne.
11. Slutsky, S. and Bertoni, H. L. (1988) 'Analysis and programmes for assessment of absorptive and tilted parallel barriers', in *Transport Research Record 1176*, National Research Council, Washington, DC.
12. May, D. and Osman, M. (1980) 'Highway noise barriers: new shapes', *Journal of Sound and Vibration*, **71**(1), 73–101.
13. Yamashita, M., Kaku, J. and Yamamoto, K. (1985) 'Net effects of absorptive acoustic barrier', in *Proceedings of Internoise 85*, Munich, pp. 507–10.
14. Clairbois, J-P. (1990) *Road and Rail Noise – Corrective Devices*. Seminar on Acoustic Noise Barriers – The Engineered Solution to Road and Rail Noise Pollution. Institute of Mechanical Engineers, London.
15. Hothersall, D. C. and Tomlinson, S. A. (1995) 'High sided vehicles and road traffic noise barriers', in *Proceedings of Internoise 95*, Newport Beach, USA, pp. 397–400.
16. Woehner, H. (1992) 'Sound propagation at tunnel openings', *Noise Control Engineering Journal*, **39**(2), 47–56.
17. Hothersall, D. C., Crombie, D. H. and Chandler-Wilde, S. N. (1991) 'The performance of T-profile and assorted noise barriers', *Applied Acoustics*, **32**, 269–87.
18. Watts, G. (1993) 'Acoustic performance of new designs of traffic noise barriers', in *Proc. Noise '93*, St Petersburg, Russia.

19. Hajeck, J. J. and Blaney, C. T. (1984) 'Evaluation of T-profile highway noise barriers', in *Transport Research Record 983*, National Research Council, Washington, DC, pp. 8–17.
20. May, D. N. and Osman, M. M. (1980) 'The performance of sound absorptive, reflective and T-profile noise barriers in Toronto', *Journal of Sound and Vibration*, **71**(1), 65–71.
21. Watts, G. R. (1996) 'Acoustic performance of a multiple edge noise barrier profile at motorway sites', *Applied Acoustics*, **42**, 47–66.
22. Shima, H., Watanabe, T., Mizuno, K., Iida, K., Matsumoto, K. and Nakasaki, K. (1996) 'Noise reduction of a multiple edge noise barrier', in *Proceedings of Internoise '96*, Liverpool, pp. 791–4.
23. Alfredson, R.J. and Du, X. (1995) 'Special shapes and treatment for noise barriers', in *Proceedings of Internoise '95*, Newport Beach, CA, pp. 381–4.
24. Fujiwara, K. and Furuta, N. (1991) 'Sound shielding efficiency of a barrier with a cylinder at the edge', *Noise Control Engineering Journal*, **37**(1), 5–11.
25. Fujiwara, K., Ohkubu, T. and Omoto, A. (1995) 'A note on the noise shielding efficiency of a barrier with absorbing obstacle at the edge', in *Proceedings of Internoise '95*, Newport Beach, CA, pp. 393–6.
26. Yamamoto, K., Shono, Y., Ochiai, H. and Yoshihiro, H. (1995) 'Measurements of noise reduction by absorptive devices mounted at the top of highway noise barriers', in *Proceedings of Internoise '95*, Newport Beach, CA, pp. 389–92.
27. Gharabegian, A. (1995) 'Improving soundwall performance using route silent', in *Proceedings of Internoise '95*, Newport Beach, CA, pp. 385–8.
28. Mizuno, K., Sekiguchi, H. and Iida, K. (1984) 'Research on a noise control device – first report, fundamental principles of the device', *Japanese Society of Mechanical Engineers*, **27**(229), 1499–505.
29. Mizuno, K., Sekiguchi, H. and Iida, K. (1985) 'Research on a noise control device – second report, fundamental design of the device', *Japanese Society of Mechanical Engineers*, **28**(245), 2737–43.
30. Iida, K., Kondoh, Y. and Okado, Y. (1984) 'Research on a device for reducing noise', in *Transport Research Record 983*, National Research Council, Washington, DC, pp. 51–4.
31. Watts, G. (1996) 'Acoustic performance of an interference-type noise-barrier profile', *Applied Acoustics*, **49**(1), 1–16.
32. Fujiwara, K. and Yotsumoto, E. (1990) 'Sound shielding efficiency of a barrier with soft surface', in *Proceedings of Internoise '90*, pp. 343–6.
33. Fujiwara, K., Hothersall, D.C. and Kim, C-H. (1996) 'Noise barriers with reactive surfaces', *Applied Acoustics*, **53**(4), 255–72.
34. Amram, M., Chvrojka, V. J. and Droin, L. (1987) 'Phase reversal barriers for better noise control at low frequencies: laboratory versus field measurements', *Noise Control Engineering Journal*, **28**(1), 16–23.
35. Gomperts, M. C. and Kihlman, T. (1968) 'The sound transmission loss of circular and slit-shaped apertures in walls', *Acustica*, **18**, 144–50.
36. Mechel, F. P. (1986) 'The acoustic sealing of holes and slits in walls', *Journal of Sound and Vibration*, **111**(2), 297–336.
37. The Transportation Research Board (1982) *Highway Noise Barriers*, National Academy of Sciences, Washington, DC, p. 15.
38. Wirt, L. S. (1979) 'The control of diffracted sound by means of thnadners (shaped noise barriers)', *Acoustica*, **42**(2), 73–88.
39. Ho, S. S. T., Busch-Vishniac, I. J. and Blackstock, D. T. (1997) 'Noise reduction by a barrier having a random edge profile', *Journal of the Acoustical Society of America*, **101**(5), pt 1, 2669–76.

40. Kragh, J. (1982) *Road Traffic Noise Attenuation by Belts of Trees and Bushes*, Report No. 31, Danish Acoustical Laboratory, Lyngby, Denmark.
41. Huddart, L. (1990) *The Use of Vegetation for Traffic Noise Screening*, Report No. 238, Transport and Road Research Laboratory, Crowthorne.
42. Martens, M. J. M. (1980) 'Foliage as a low pass filter: experiments with model forests in an anechoic chamber', in Martens, M. J. M. (ed.) *Geluid en Groen*, Katholieke Universiteit, Nijmegen, Netherlands, pp. 118–40.
43. Cook, D. I. and Van Haverbeke, D. F. (1974) *Tree Covered Landforms for Noise Control*, Research Bulletin 263, The Forest Service, US Department of Agriculture, Washington, DC.
44. European Committee for Standardization (1997) *EN 1793–1 Road Traffic Reducing Devices – Test Method for Determining the Acoustic Performance – Part 1: Intrinsic Characteristics of Sound Absorption*, CEN, Brussels.
45. European Committee for Standardization (1997) *EN 1793–1 Road Traffic Reducing Devices – Test Method for Determining the Acoustic Performance – Part 2: Intrinsic Characteristics of Airborne Sound Insulation*, CEN, Brussels.
46. European Committee for Standardization (1997) *EN 1793–1 Road Traffic Reducing Devices – Test Method for Determining the Acoustic Performance – Part 3: Normalized Traffic Noise Spectrum*, CEN, Brussels.

Barrier morphology and design

4

Anatomy of barriers – elements and characteristics

It has been necessary to create a simple morphology for barriers in order to describe their component parts and analyse the elements that help to make or break their aesthetic appeal. With this tool it is possible to describe barriers, directing attention towards their individual elements and clarifying why some barriers are more visually appealing or satisfactory than others.

Essentially, barrier morphology, or the classification of the form and structures relating to barriers, is uncomplicated, as barriers are generally made up of a small number of essential parts. A barrier may be seen to have a top section, a middle section, and a base section, even if perhaps it is constructed out of a single uniform material. It also has a top edge which provides a silhouette against its background, a bottom edge where it meets the surrounding ground, a support structure and foundations (Figure 4.1).

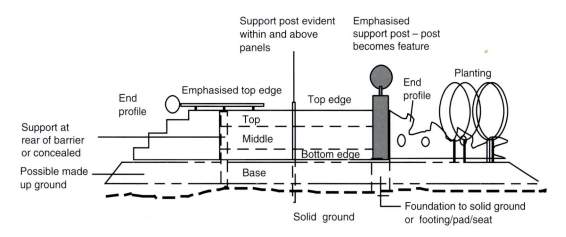

4.1 Barrier morphology

Top section and top edge

The top section and edge of the barrier are critical to its visual appeal and appearance when seen against the landscape/townscape backdrop. For a pedestrian, with an average eye level of approximately 1.5–1.7 m, the top of a barrier is nearly always going to be above eye level. This means that, more often than not, the top edge of the barrier will be silhouetted against the sky, a backdrop of vegetation or perhaps against buildings and other built forms. In a car, eye-level is considerably lower, at approximately 1.3–1.4 m, and thus barriers are always likely to be viewed upwards. The background against which the barrier will be viewed is, therefore, an important consideration and it is essential to ascertain whether the visual and aesthetic strategy calls for losing the top edge of the barrier within the landscape, or alternatively providing some strength to the edge so that it makes a more dominant visual statement (Figures 4.2 and 4.3).

Usually the answer depends upon the location of the barrier. Generally there are two main scenarios, countryside and cityscape. In the countryside or in rural areas, experience has indicated that barriers should be concealed, or appear transparent and as lightweight as possible in the landscape. The top section and top edge should fade or blend easily into the backdrop of the sky or vegetation. This may also be the case in urban areas where many successful barriers use transparent and lighter materials at the top to reduce the overall apparent height of the barrier and to allow light to pass through (Figure 4.4).

However, in urban areas, where there is often a jumble of built forms and a clutter of urban paraphernalia, such as signage, poles and lighting, with a juxtaposition of often discordant materials, a barrier with strength of form and a firm and distinctive silhouette may be better suited. In these situations, a well-designed barrier may help to strengthen the urban structure, whereas a visually weak one may have the reverse effect and add to visual clutter and discordance (Figure 4.5).

The treatment of the top edge may, however, be dictated by acoustic considerations rather than aesthetic ones, because the diffraction of noise at the top edge may be better controlled by a number of proprietary devices.

4.2 Non-acoustic element forming a top edge

4.3 The visual image of a barrier is the sum of the barrier and its background

4.4 Transparent and light-coloured materials reduce the visual impact of a barrier

4.5 Assertive design elements can enhance the cityscape, Docklands Light Railway

These systems generally involve the use of sound-absorbing elements such as the bulbous-mushroom form developed in Japan (see Figure 3.18) or additional diffracting edges. All of these devices add to the bulk of the top edge of the barrier and require particular attention to ensure that they are visually acceptable.

Middle section

The middle section, or body, of the barrier is likely to form the major visually apparent part of the barrier, as it will usually be largest section and will probably mitigate most of the views. This is also because the principles of

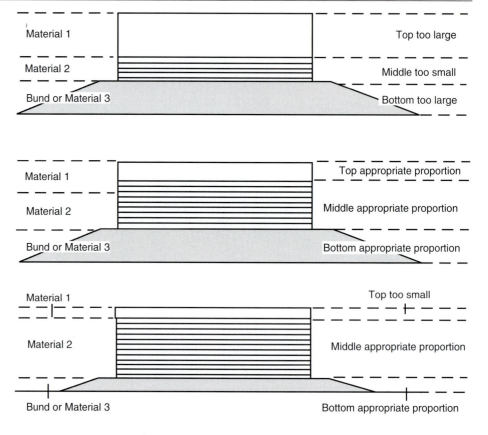

4.6 Barrier proportions

Note: When the top of the barrier is of a different material a more aesthetic appearance is usually achieved if it is 20–30% of the vertical barrier height

proportion in design suggest that the barrier should not appear top or bottom heavy. The whole of the barrier needs to be considered, including the rise and fall in the topography and the incorporation of earth embankments and mounds. In many cases, a barrier may comprise a single uniform facade of a single material, but what is below the barrier, namely the ground or the earth, is likely to form part of the complete barrier. Thus, many barriers in rural or semirural locations comprise an arrangement of earth mounding with a vertical section on top. The visual complexity of this arrangement may be further complicated by the addition of other materials, say a transparent section on top, which will lighten the appearance of the barrier and potentially reduce its visual impact. Ideally, to avoid visual clutter and disharmony, the middle section of the barrier should only comprise a single material, although this may, of course, be subject to changes in form and/or colour (Figure 4.6).

Bottom section and bottom edge

The bottom edge of a barrier may in reality be obscured by planting, grasses or perhaps by a kerb or safety fence. In the past it has been seen to be essential that this section is designed and constructed without gaps or holes through

4.7 Raised planters provide horticultural and visual benefits

which noise can pass. There are now some cases in the Netherlands where gaps are being left at the bottom of barriers so that no special drainage is required, and so that smaller animals may pass through. Maintenance costs are also reduced as there is no contact between the soil and the barrier and therefore there is less corrosion.

The base also needs to be in an appropriate proportion to the sections of barrier above. Many barriers utilise planters within the bottom section. This helps to give weight and visual complexity to the barrier without it being overrefined, as well as removing the planting mixture away from contaminants such as salt used to de-ice roads in winter and from heavy metal pollution from exhausts which tend to gravitate downwards to the road or kerb level (Figure 4.7). This section is also where water may collect and may contain areas for road drainage. Thus, the designer needs to be aware of potential maintenance operations within the transport corridor and of the barrier itself. The appropriate measures must be incorporated within the design to accommodate these issues.

Barrier façades

A barrier also has two façades: the front or side which faces the traffic and the back or public side which faces the protected area. In some cases these may be treated similarly, but in most cases, the front elevation differs from the rear elevation because the barrier usually mitigates noise from only one direction. The front of a barrier may also be different from the back because of the need for supports, which in many instances are placed to the rear. In many cases this difference is also due to other construction techniques and cost, but usually it is due to a combination of factors. Most importantly, however, the visual quality and character of the front and back needs to reflect the visual quality and character of the particular surroundings which may differ on

4.8 Front side of barrier visually reflects the motorway corridor

4.9 Rear side of barrier visually softened for residents

either side. One side of the barrier may not be as important as the other, where, for example, the barrier itself may be screened by vegetation, or where it is hidden from view. Figures 4.8 and 4.9 show the front and rear elevations of a barrier near Milan in Italy. Whereas the front facade is faced with a perforated aluminium skin, timber has been applied to the rear to soften the appearance of the barrier for the people living next to it. The effect would be further improved by planting, however.

Ends

It must be stated that the barrier needs to be at its total designed height along all of its length to achieve its acoustic and visual screening objectives. Any end detail, such as tapering, must extend beyond the end point of the functional design of the barrier. Thus, whereas the design of the main façade of a barrier often concerns a dialectic between the landscape architect and

4.10 Three additional end panels are used to visually terminate the barrier

the acoustic engineer over different requirements and ideals, the design of the barrier termination is essentially an aesthetic consideration and is not generally an acoustic issue. It is usually an 'add on' to the full length and height required for the main barrier (Figure 4.10).

The visual transition between a route corridor without a barrier to a corridor with a barrier and *vice versa*, such as between an open space and a visually contained space, may be awkward and therefore needs to be treated sensitively. There are two opposite ways of dealing with this situation, namely to highlight these ends or to downplay or disguise the ends. The simplest way of disguising the beginning and end of a barrier is to envelop it in planting, but it would be visually more pleasing if this planting related to other planting along the length of the barrier as well. This other planting could be located where there is an awkward height transition or a deviation in alignment (Figure 4.11).

In most cases, well-designed barriers in rural and semirural areas do not appear to just stop dead, although some examples show that this may be a visually effective and robust feature. Most barriers tend to taper, step down or break up when they start or finish. In more urban locations the ending of a barrier is usually more abrupt and visually acceptable. An appropriate

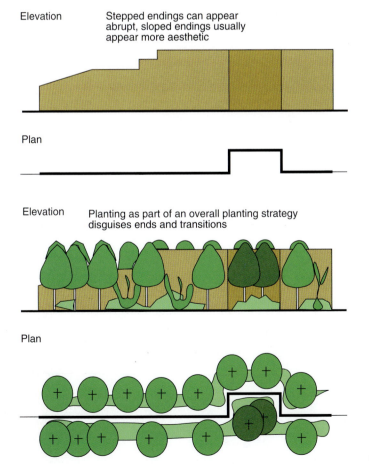

Elevation   Stepped endings can appear abrupt, sloped endings usually appear more aesthetic

Plan

Elevation   Planting as part of an overall planting strategy disguises ends and transitions

Plan

4.11 Barrier ends and transitions

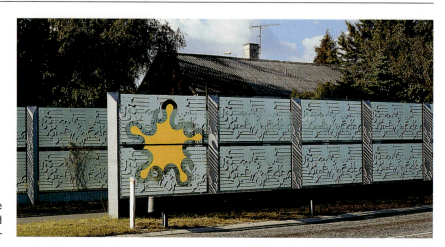

4.12 A visual highlight to the end of a visually sophisticated semitransparent glass barrier

4.13 Successfully terminated timber absorptive barrier using a sloping end

4.14 An abrupt ending adds a sense of contemporaneity to this high-tech aluminium and transparent barrier

appearance may be achieved by the use of a feature which integrates well with the overall barrier design (Figures 4.12, 4.13 and 4.14).

Vertical profile – angled and cantilevered barriers

The vertical profile of a barrier is, of course, an essential consideration. If the barrier comprises an earth mound, it is the angle of repose of the earth that forms its profile. If the barrier is made of rigid components, then these may be erected either vertically, or at an angle, or in a partially concave or cantilevered shape.

The profile of an earth mound can give the impression of a highly engineered situation if it is steep, has crisp lines and is characterised by visually simple planting, such as grass or groundcovers (Figure 4.15). In contrast to this, where mound profiles are eased and where edges are less defined and varied, or where planting is more complex with shrubs and trees in non-defined patterns, the mound will appear much more naturalistic (Figure 4.16). In fact, in such cases, the mound may not be seen as a mound at all, but

4.15 Simple ornamental planting provides definition and character to a mound

4.16 Naturalistic planting integrates an earth mound into the rural landscape

give the impression that the transport corridor has proceeded into a cutting. The use of mounding on both sides of a transport corridor is often referred to as a false cutting.

The angle of a barrier not only has an effect on the direction of the noise it is reflecting, but it also has important aesthetic effects. If a barrier has a vertical profile, it appears to be and may be understood to be a wall or a fence. If the barrier is angled it suggests that it is something else, that it is a noise barrier. Moreover, viewing a vertical barrier from within a road corridor usually gives an impression of confinement. This impression is eased by the angling of a barrier outwards, which tends to open up the view above and beyond. This impression also depends on the form, colour and top profile of the barrier. In order to reduce this impression of confinement it is recommended that the top profile of the barrier is kept simple and it is even better if the top section is transparent. Viewing an angled barrier closely from outside a road corridor, where the top of the barrier is angled towards the viewer, may also present a feeling of confinement and claustrophobia. For this reason, it is recommended that, should there be public access immediately to the rear of a barrier, it should not be angled. If, however, the barrier is not immediately adjacent to public access then angling of the barrier may be considered (Figure 4.17).

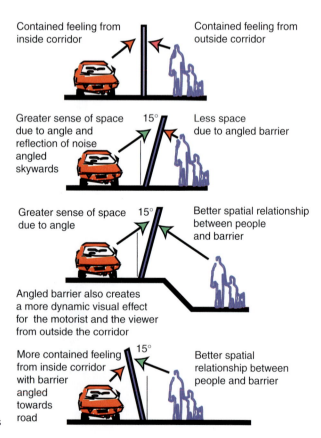

4.17 Angled barriers and spatial effects

Contained feeling from inside corridor

Contained feeling from outside corridor

Greater sense of space due to angle and reflection of noise angled skywards

15°

Less space due to angled barrier

Greater sense of space due to angle

15°

Better spatial relationship between people and barrier

Angled barrier also creates a more dynamic visual effect for the motorist and the viewer from outside the corridor

More contained feeling from inside corridor with barrier angled towards road

15°

Better spatial relationship between people and barrier

4.18 Angled barriers appear dynamic

4.19 Splayed barrier makes a virtue out of an engineering necessity

On the whole, angled barriers tend to have a more dynamic and designed appearance and tend to make more of a visual statement (Figure 4.18). Some barriers have been angled out of physical necessity. Most angled barriers are tilted 3–15° from the vertical, depending on the materials and supports used, the height of barrier and the local surroundings. An example of this is the TGV rail line in Paris where a continuous barrier has been required: the ingenious use of intermittent angling allows gantries to be accommodated harmoniously into the design. This concertina effect adds important visual complexity to the barrier in an already complex visual setting and creates a strong design statement (Figure 4.19).

Cantilevered barriers are made in a range of shapes and sizes depending on their function. In most cases, however, a cantilevered barrier will reduce visual impact from outside the road corridor by easing or blurring the top edge of the barrier when viewed against the sky. This can also be achieved by using transparent sections at the top of the barrier (Figure 4.20). Cantilevering can also effectively reduce the height of barriers by moving part of the barrier closer to the noise source. These overhangs may be extremely large and bold, but in many cases they are visually quite subtle. The decision to use

Normal opaque barrier

Full height of barrier faces viewer

Normal opaque barrier with transparent top section

Apparent height of barrier reduced due to light appearance of top transparent section

Partially cantilevered curved barrier

Top part of barrier curves away from viewer reducing apparent height

Partially cantilevered curved barrier with transparent top

Top part of barrier curves away from viewer and top transparent section reducing apparent height

Partially cantilevered angled barrier

Top part of barrier angled away from viewer reducing apparent height

Partially cantilevered angled barrier with transparent top

Top part of barrier curves away from viewer and top transparent section reducing apparent height

Angled barrier

Barrier angled away from viewer and top catches more light therefore reducing apparent height.
Note: Opposite effect on other side

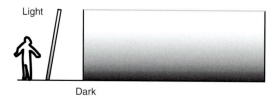

4.20 Reducing apparent barrier heights

*Note: Angled or rounded transparent sections may appear partially opaque if viewed at a tangent to the transparent section. Face-on views offer the best transparency.

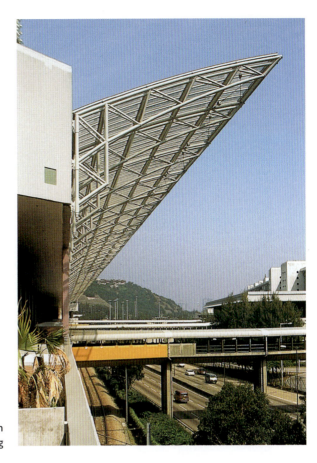

4.21 Elegant cantilevered barrier 20 m high and 8 m wide protects residential tower blocks in Hong Kong

4.22 Public open space preserved by using a cantilevered barrier, Hong Kong

4.23 Dynamic appearance achieved by cantilevered aluminium barriers, Bellinzona, Switzerland

4.24 Substantial pre-stressed concrete support structure for cantilevered barrier, Dordrecht, the Netherlands (see Figures 4.33, 5.62 and 5.63)

4.25 (above) The structure is the dominant visual element, Gouda Railway Station, the Netherlands

4.26 (opposite) The bold structure is incorporated into an overall design concept

a cantilevered barrier is usually based on acoustic as well as visual or aesthetic criteria, i.e. keeping the barrier as low as possible to reduce visual impact from outside the road/rail corridor while also reducing noise. A cantilevered barrier also appears more dynamic from within a transport corridor, especially where that corridor includes bends or curves. Cost is also an important consideration as supports and foundations may need to be more robust and complex (Figures 4.21–4.24).

Support structures, transitions and foundations

As with any architectural form, the structure of a barrier may be used as a functional as well as an aesthetic element. The structure may then have an important visual function, which helps to define the character of the barrier. This emphasis on the structure can of course vary from a minimal expression to a bold expression where the structure itself becomes the dominant visual element (Figures 4.25 and 4.26). Supports can also be appropriate or inappropriate in the context of their surroundings (Figure 4.27).

Like many of the other elements of the barrier, the structure which supports the barrier requires the consideration of all of the design team. It is the structure supporting the barrier that can be subjected to significant stresses, especially wind loading, and must be designed to meet the appropriate engineering requirements. However, the design of the structure is also an important aesthetic consideration and it can either be emphasised, or down-played, or even concealed within the facade to give a seamless appearance to the barrier (Figures 4.28 and 4.29). However, it should be borne in mind that the latter structures may appear monotonous unless other features are used to alleviate the uniformity of the barrier surface. A continuous undifferentiated surface may also simply be produced by using reinforced concrete produced within rolling formwork. Potentially this can produce a visually blunt and heavy barrier which offers a tantalising surface for graffiti artists. Where there is a risk of graffiti it is prudent to use profiled or textured surfaces and use the structure to break up the regular surface (Figures 4.30 and 4.31).

4.27 The scale and design of concrete posts appear inappropriate against a natural backdrop

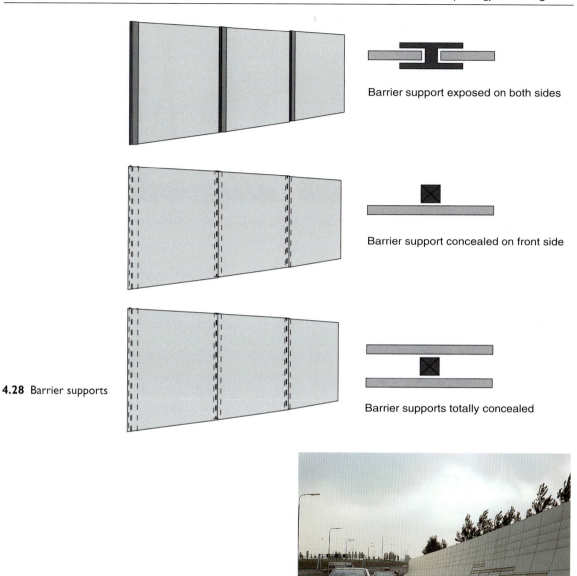

Barrier support exposed on both sides

Barrier support concealed on front side

4.28 Barrier supports

Barrier supports totally concealed

4.29 A seamless appearance of aluminium presents a high-tech image, A10, Amsterdam

In most instances, apart from earth mounds and bio-barriers, the barrier is formed from panels which are positioned between vertical posts. These posts are either fixed below ground onto piles, or set within, or bolted onto a concrete foundation (Figure 4.32). The number of vertical supports can be minimised by using lateral support structures either above or behind the barrier (Figure 4.33).

4.30 Grafitti artists find bland even surfaces irresistible

4.31 Even well-executed grafitti will not enhance a barrier

The use of posts is avoided altogether in a recent development, in which precast panels are bolted directly onto the foundations (Figure 4.34).

New advances in planar glazing have added variety to the support of transparent glazed barriers, where the glass panels are supported by a series of posts, arms and cables (Figure 4.35).

Where more than a single or uniform material is used within the vertical or horizontal profile of a barrier, the transition is also an important visual consideration. Even when very different materials are used, a harmonious transition may be achieved by carrying elements from one section of the barrier into the other. Aesthetically this should also create a satisfactory transition, but on the traffic corridor side these transitions tend to blur because the barrier is viewed at speed. Yet this transition can be used as a design element and, if it is not considered as such, the visual quality of the barrier may be degraded (Figure 4.36).

The ground itself, and its geotechnical make-up are important considerations and the foundations of a barrier may need to be quite substantial, if for example, a barrier is positioned on a road embankment, which may be of made-up ground. In such cases, deep piles which reach below the made-up ground may be required, together with ground anchors, to support the structure. The foundations can thus add considerably to the cost of the proposals. The foundations are critically important as the barrier may be subject to extreme wind loading. They will also have to be integrated with the road drainage system.

Fixings

Fixings are important elements, especially from cost, weathering, maintenance and replacement considerations. Fixings should allow the barrier to be fitted into place easily and allow for the easy removal and replacement of damaged panels or units. The issue of replacing panels is an important aesthetic consideration. It has been found to be worthwhile to manufacture and store additional panels where there is a risk that some of these may, over time, be damaged. Thus, when a barrier becomes damaged, it

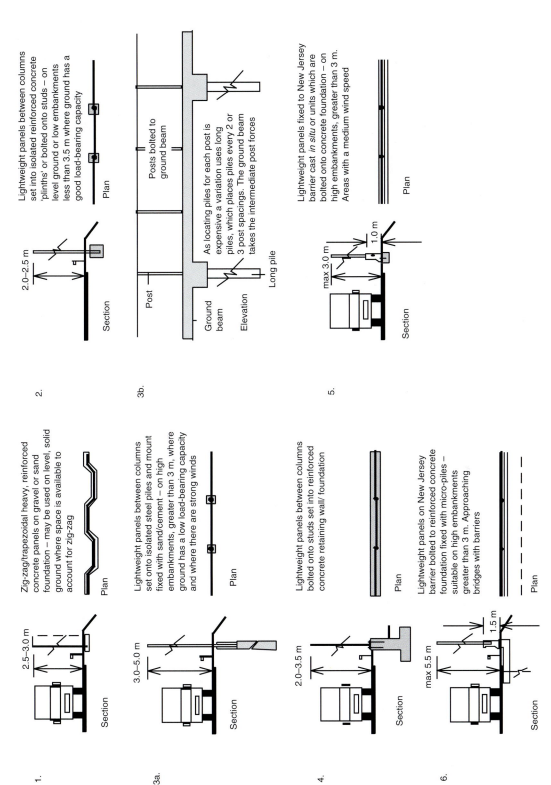

1.
Zig-zag/trapezoidal heavy, reinforced concrete panels on gravel or sand foundation – may be used on level, solid ground where space is available to account for zig-zag

2.5–3.0 m
Section
Plan

2.
Lightweight panels between columns set into isolated reinforced concrete 'plinths' or bolted onto studs – on level ground or low embankments less than 3.5 m where ground has a good load-bearing capacity

2.0–2.5 m
Section
Plan

3a.
Lightweight panels between columns set onto isolated steel piles and mount fixed with sand/cement – on high embankments, greater than 3 m, where ground has a low load-bearing capacity and where there are strong winds

3.0–5.0 m
Section
Plan

3b.
Posts bolted to ground beam

As locating piles for each post is expensive a variation uses long piles, which places piles every 2 or 3 post spacings. The ground beam takes the intermediate post forces

Post
Ground beam
Long pile
Elevation

4.
Lightweight panels between columns bolted onto studs set into reinforced concrete retaining wall/ foundation

2.0–3.5 m
Section
Plan

5.
Lightweight panels fixed to New Jersey barrier cast in situ or units which are bolted onto concrete foundation – on high embankments, greater than 3 m. Areas with a medium wind speed

max 3.0 m
1.0 m
Section
Plan

6.
Lightweight panels on New Jersey barrier bolted to reinforced concrete foundation fixed with micro-piles – suitable on high embankments greater than 3 m. Approaching bridges with barriers

max 5.5 m
1.5 m
Section
Plan

4.32 Barrier foundation types (information derived, in part, from OECD[1])

4.33 Steel lattice structure used to maximise the distance between support posts

4.34 A modular panel from a postless absorptive granular concrete barrier system, Milan, Italy

will be less costly to replace like with like; also, it will be easier to maintain the intended appearance of the barrier.

Other considerations

Viewing at speed

The factor of speed is an important consideration affecting the total design of the barrier. For the motorist or train passenger, the barrier is most often seen at speed, although the motorist has longer forward views than the train passenger, who has mainly close side-on views. In general, this means that the appearance of barriers and hence their design and construction needs to be simple, with clean lines and edges. Small nuances and changes in pattern, colour or texture are likely to be lost and in fact may create visual disharmony as they blur into a visual clutter. However, barriers are not only seen at speed; they often dissect areas in constant use by local residents. The barrier design, therefore, needs to take account of their views as well as harmonising with the overall design and character of the urban fabric. In this respect, it is extremely important to stress that the barrier is not an independent structure which is designed only in its own right. It must tie in with the character of the transport corridor as well as into the local surroundings. This is, of course, the most critical issue, apart from the acoustic considerations. Each barrier, and each façade of the barrier, needs to be considered with regard to the local environment.

Two-faced barriers

It is not common for both sides of a barrier to look identical because it is usually only one side of the barrier which is required to reflect or absorb noise. The difference between the two sides of a barrier should be determined on aesthetic as well as acoustic reasons: each side of the barrier should be

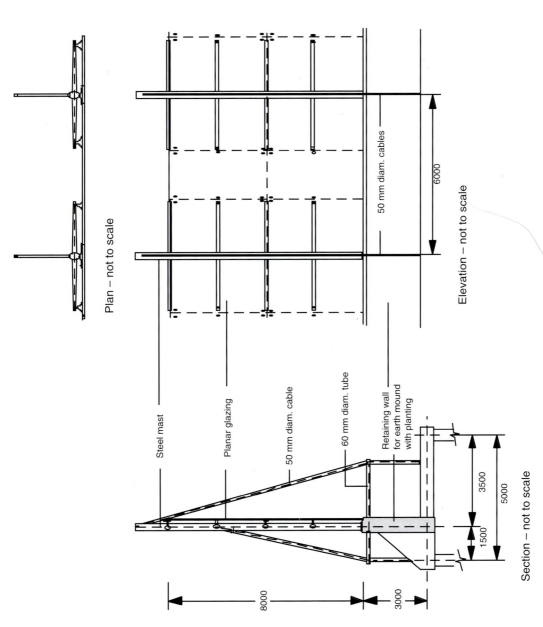

Plan – not to scale

Elevation – not to scale

50 mm diam. cables

6000

Steel mast

Planar glazing

50 mm diam. cable

60 mm diam. tube

Retaining wall
for earth mound
with planting

Section – not to scale

8000

3000

3500

5000

1500

4.35 Noise barrier with planar glazing (after Building Design Partnership and Benz Kotzen)

4.36 The repetition of vertical and horizontal design elements is used to achieve a harmonious transition between two systems

designed to integrate with the landscape character, and the backdrop against which it is to be viewed. Thus the face of the barrier that may be facing a road corridor may include a pattern or have a bright colour, whereas the other face, which could stand opposite housing may be treated in a more discreet fashion. Here the façade may be plain and designed to merge in with adjacent planting. Most barrier types can be designed with this in mind with the obvious exceptions of transparent barriers and many bio-barriers. Planting on either side of the barrier should also be designed with each separate identity in mind.

There are, however, many exceptions where road and rail corridors run side by side, which require both sides of the barrier to reduce noise. This may also occur where central reservation barriers are required between road carriage-ways. In these instances the barrier, which is usually designed to absorb noise, may appear similar from either side. But even here, both sides of the barrier need to be assessed relative to the surrounding landscape.

Another important consideration is the provision and maintenance of views into the landscape for motorists and rail passengers, and in this regard it may be appropriate to design barriers which allow views towards the landscape. This may conflict with the needs of those whom the barrier is intended to protect (Figure 4.37). Although the research for this book has not revealed a barrier incorporating one-way glass, this may be an appropriate solution in situations where views out from the transport corridor are desirable and where views into the transport corridor may be unwanted. This can also be achieved by assessing the major views out and towards the corridor and then by designing kick-back windows or staggered panels which allow glimpses out but which restrict views in (Figure 4.38). Figures 4.39 and 5.49 show how staggering can greatly reduce the visual impact of a barrier and allow views out of the road corridor, but unfortunately in this case the views are directly into a private garden.

Barriers: Vertical or horizontal landscape elements?

Generally, barriers may be considered as horizontal elements in the landscape because the horizontal dimension is usually much greater than the vertical. In some cases, however, the vertical dimension is just as impressive as is

View from the road/rail line:
transparent barrier allows views to the landscape creating interest for driver and passengers

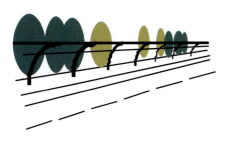

View from the road/rail line:
Transparent barrier allows views to road/rail traffic which may be disturbing to local inhabitants and amenity users

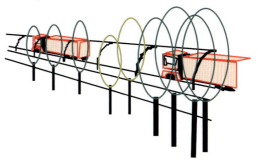

View from the road/rail line:
Opaque barrier stops views to landscape creating an enclosed transport corridor insulated from the interest of the landscape

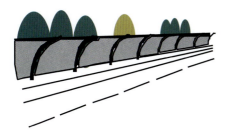

View from the road/rail line:
Opaque barrier stops views to road/rail traffic creating a more peaceful character. But in some areas the movement of traffic may add visual interest. There may also be long views of interest which are blocked although the near distance views of traffic are mitigated

4.37 Some advantages and disadvantages of transparent barriers

evidenced by the 20 m high barrier which protects housing areas alongside the Périphérique in Paris (see Figure 1.1).

Emphasising the vertical elements of a barrier may be an appropriate way of making a visual statement and a means of creating visual continuity and rhythm. However, there is a danger of using these elements in the wrong context, as they can appear out of place or character and be visually intrusive, especially if viewed against a natural backdrop. Cute and visually obvious solutions can appear trite and can quickly become outdated. Vertical elements can be used to serve a real visual function, for example, by directing attention to the location of the escape doors, but, even in such cases, this can be overdone (Figure 4.40).

Repetition

Barrier design is generally based on the repetition of panels and structure. This strategy is important in keeping costs down and providing visual

1. Straight barrier:
Transparent sections allow views,
opaque sections prohibit views

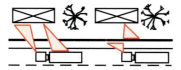

4. Straight barrier with occasional windows:
Transparent sections allow partial views,
opaque sections prohibit views

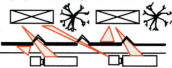

2. Staggered barrier:
Transparent sections allow views,
opaque sections prohibit views

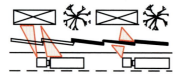

5. Staggered offset barrier:
Transparent sections allow views,
opaque sections prohibit views

3. Zig-zag barrier:
Transparent sections allow partial views,
opaque sections prohibit views

6. Staggered stepped barrier:
Small transparent sections allow partial views,
opaque sections prohibit views

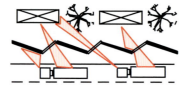

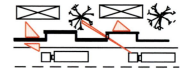

NOTE:
• Barriers with transparent sections can benefit drivers and passengers by allowing views out but may disadvantage local people.

• Barriers 3,4 and 6 limit views to the traffic corridor but allow some views from the corridor thereby creating interest for the driver and passengers.

4.38 Barrier arrangements – opacity versus transparency

continuity, but it can risk introducing or creating visually boring elements into the landscape. Such barriers can also alter the landscape character of an area and diminish landscape quality. Most barriers designed today follow one or more of four principal design approaches:

• to provide a simple barrier with no variety or material differentiation, or focal points along its length;

• to provide periodic focal points or features along the length of the barrier;

• to allow for a pattern within the overall façade of the barrier, such as staggered windows, or a change in material;

4.39 Staggered pvc barrier with intermediate windows at right angles opens up views for the traveller

4.40 Pagoda structure draws attention to an escape door

- to provide visual variety by moving the horizontal alignment of the barrier away from and towards the transport corridor, by creating dog-legs, curves and splays.

Pattern

Applied patterns or patterns of light and shade created by barrier elements are an important tool in the designer's palette, but pattern should be used with due care. Patterns, if too simple, can appear stark, contrived and even puerile. Patterning, where required, needs to be sophisticated and bold. If it is too subtle it may be lost when viewed at speed. Pattern should also be an

4.41 Visual interest created by a bas-relief pattern

integral part of, and relate to, the form and elements of the construction; surface treatments and painted patterns rarely appear successful. Patterns created in bas-relief work with light and shade and are usually more visually sophisticated (Figure 4.41).

Texture

The texture of a barrier is essentially defined by the material make-up of the barrier, although in many cases, when travelling at speed, or when viewed from a distance, the textural nature of the material can appear indistinct. The texture of the material, therefore, should not affect the visual quality of the barrier except where close views are possible. Thus, for example, the porous nature of a concreted wood-fibre barrier or an absorptive brick barrier is lost, except when viewed close up (Figures 4.42 and 4.43). Absorptive metal barriers generally appear as reflective metal barriers when viewed from any distance. Timber barriers also have their own definitive appearance and texture, and in the UK they generally have a distinct 'garden fence' quality. In continental Europe timber is used in a variety of ways to provide a range of textures, colours and a play of light and shade (Figure 4.44). The textural effects of planting can also help to provide visual interest and complexity (Figure 4.45).

Furthermore, it must be emphasised that combining materials, textures and/or colours is of critical importance: usually a maximum of two should be used, not including that of the support structure. This may be increased to three, if planting is included as the third texture.

Colour

Colour is obviously one of the most important character-defining criteria for any architectural element and is critical in determining the visual character and quality of the barrier. One of the interesting and challenging problems with colour in temperate zones is the changes of season. This is particularly an issue in rural locations where a colour chosen to blend into its surroundings in summer, may stand out like a sore thumb during the winter months. It is, therefore, not surprising that in many cases, the choice of colour is

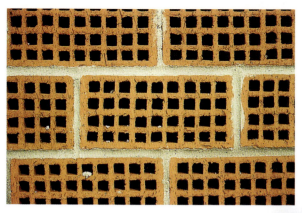

4.42 Textural detail of an absorptive brick barrier

4.43 Texture becomes a less significant factor with distant views

4.44 Colour, form, light and shade combine to add interest to a timber-absorptive barrier

4.45 Planting helps to provide visual interest

4.46 Well-conceived use of strong colours

4.47 Burgundy tones work surprisingly well

4.48 Well-designed transparent barrier using grey–blue transparent panels. Red posts enhance the old bridge structure

inappropriate. Colour, like any other design criterion, should be chosen for a particular reason and not be chosen arbitrarily, or simply because it is available. Colour, as with texture, can also be determined by the material, although this can be changed through the application of paints, stains and anodising. A metallic colour, such as the silver sheen of aluminium gives a quality, high-tech engineered appearance. Muted green colours and timber colours give the effect of nature and the natural environment. Bright colours, such as reds and yellows and oranges imply conscious design and the making of a statement. Thus, colouring parts of a barrier red, for example, states that the barrier has some visual/architectural merit and in such cases care should be taken to make sure that this statement is justified. Bright colours are used to both good and bad effect in urban and suburban locations, but they are rarely successful in rural locations. It may be a function of present-day fashion, but it appears that in the UK and the rest of Europe, muted noncontrived colours and tones appear to work well in most urban locations. Whites and off-whites, concrete shades, greys, the light and shade of glass, metallic sheens and muted colours appear to fit in and are easy on the eye. An exception, where bright colours do work visually, is found where the total design is well conceived (Figure 4.46). In rural and semirural locations muted tones also appear pleasing. Glass, timber tones, tawny browns and olive and oaky greens and some greys appear tranquil. It is also surprising to note that some darker russet and burgundy tones appear satisfactory and do not jar the eye as might be expected (Figure 4.47).

Care must also be used when selecting coloured transparent elements. Slight tints of grey and blue usually appear satisfactory as they reflect the colours of the sky (Figure 4.48). Rose and beige tinted glass can appear dull and lifeless in the landscape. The occasional use of brightly coloured glass can be a very effective design element (Figure 4.49). Additionally, the occasional use of a bright colour, which highlights a specific architectural feature, can lift the appearance of the overall design (Figure 4.50).

In many instances colour and tone are graded from dark at the bottom of the barrier to light at the top, where it may be viewed against a lighter sky. Generally, this is visually pleasing, especially where the colour gradations are balanced and subtle. Ambitious colour changes appear to be stark, ill-fitting and contrived, unless they are part of a visually robust and complex urban setting (Figure 4.51).

In Switzerland, Swiss Federal Railways has chosen a particular dark-grey colour for all of its absorptive barriers. This colour is effective in that it reflects, to a great extent, the colours of the railway environment, including the greys of the steel tracks, rolling stock, gantries, concrete sleepers and the granite ballast that holds the sleepers and tracks in place. The colour was chosen for all barriers so as to provide a particular corporate image and thus, when such a barrier is seen, it says 'Swiss Federal Railways'. In many respects the chosen colour is correct and the corporate identity argument appears logical. However, the factors of light and shade and the character of individual locations have largely been ignored. This undoubtedly means that although some barriers fit neatly and sensitively into the environment, others do not (Figure 4.52).

4.49 Spots of colour lift the overall design

4.50 Striking colour used as part of an overall design concept

4.51 Robust colour used to enhance a visually complex urban setting

4.52 Swiss Federal Railways corporate barriers protecting an urban environment

Light and shade

The fall of light onto the barrier and shade created by angles, appendages, material make-up, posts and supports and vegetation constitute an important visual element and are as important as colour or texture.

In choosing a barrier and its overall design and colour, it would be well to note the aspect of the barrier and whether it will receive sunlight or whether it would be in shade or partial shade. Thus, a barrier which runs alongside a north–south transport corridor may well receive bright sunlight on one side and be in deep shadow at different times of the day, whereas a barrier located alongside a corridor on an east–west alignment may have one face always in shadow. The colour of the side of the barrier in perpetual shadow may well need to be lighter in colour to achieve the desired visual effect.

Light falling on a barrier can also create pleasing effects, which alter according to the strength of the changing light, the weather, the angle of the sun, time of day, etc. This allows a barrier to become more visually complex and interesting, especially when placed in urban locations where views are most likely to be from close up and for longer periods of time. Visual complexity is important in these locations in order to avoid visual sterility (Figure 4.53).

Profiling

Profiling, or the repeated raising and pushing back of the barrier surface, is an important consideration for absorptive barriers, as the increased surface area of the barrier can enhance the sound absorption. Profiled barriers also have the advantage of making it difficult for graffiti artists to paint coherently and therefore they are dissuaded from using surfaces which are irregular. Profiled barriers are also visually more interesting because their appearance changes throughout the day. Light highlights the peaks of the profiling at some times of the day, while causing shadows in the troughs (Figure 4.54).

4.53 The cast of light and shade adds visual complexity to galvanised steel columns

4.54 Profiling adds interest to a potentially bland surface

Materials and design

Historically, noise barrier designers have often used the palette and techniques of the architect. A barrier was seen to be a façade, just like any façade of a building. Today, however, many barriers have a particular character which allows their form to integrate with their function. Contemporary fashion dictates that verity is applauded and artifice is derided, so barriers appear to be more honest if they do not try to hide their function through trite patterning or *trompe l'oeil*. Where a noise barrier is likely to be a visual feature in the landscape it should be designed with integrity and regard to its form and function, although over time this fashion may well change. Barriers should thus be designed using the best expertise, technology and materials available, so that they fit well into the late twentieth-century *oeuvre* and will stand the test of time, at least for their design life of 40 years.

The two main reasons as to why barriers appear incongruous or characterless in the landscape or in urban locations are function and cost. Although there is no doubt that function is the primary reason for building a barrier, this should not be done to the detriment of the landscape and visual context. The function of reducing noise and/or visual intrusion must be seen in the context of the overall visual effects and impacts. In the UK, all too often it appears that off-the-shelf products are used, provided they fulfil the task of reducing the noise to the specified level. Some design may take place, but this does little to reduce the visual effects caused by the selection of inappropriate materials and does little to maintain and protect the quality of the environment. Even if token screen planting and mounding is provided, it cannot disguise a poor design. Barriers should only be designed once studies of the local natural environment have been carried out, including studies of materials, built forms and massing, colour and vegetative patterns and the historical context. Once this is completed, concepts should be explored that explain the designers' reasons for the visual appearance of the barrier.

The arrangement of planting, maintenance and safety zones alongside the barrier also needs to be considered, as this contributes to the overall visual impression. These zones may, of course, overlap and widths may vary according to the location, and the type of barrier or road (Figure 4.55).

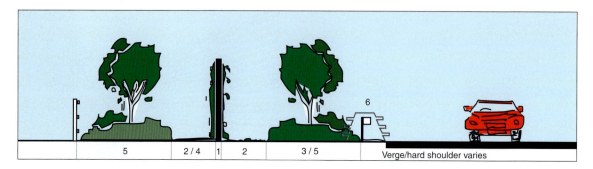

| 5 | 2 / 4 | 1 | 2 | 3 / 5 | Verge/hard shoulder varies |

Horizontal alignment: Potential arrangement 1

1.   Barrier with climbers.

2.   Maintenance zone – may vary depending on type and height of barrier – usually at least 1m on either side. May be soft or hard surface depending on location. May require drainage below ground. Climbers may be included in this area.

3.   Safety zone to the front of the barrier. Safety fence may be required depending on the vertical alignment of barrier and the distance of the barrier from the carriageway and the road standard.
Steps over safety fence may be required at periodic intervals and at escape doors.

4.   Safety zone to the rear of the barrier to allow travellers to move out of the road corridor via an escape door.
This will probably tie in with the maintenance zone.

5.   Planting zone – may vary depending on need to integrate barrier, height of barrier and materials and overall landscape strategy/concept and available space. Position of boundary fence varies depending on who is responsible for the maintenance of the planting. If a fence is required then this should be chosen to tie in with the overall landscape scheme.

6.   Safety fence may be required depending on vertical alignment of barrier and the distance of the barrier from the carriageway.

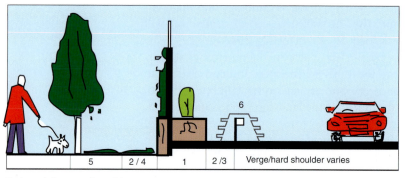

| 5 | 2 / 4 | 1 | 2 /3 | Verge/hard shoulder varies |

Horizontal alignment: Potential arrangement 2

1.   Barrier with planter and hedge – planter with climbers and climbing frame or wires.

2.   Maintenance zone for barrier and escape zone from road behind safety fence.

3.   Safety zone to the front of the barrier. Safety fence may be required depending on vertical alignment of barrier and the distance of the barrier from the carriageway.
Steps over safety fence may be required at periodic intervals.

4.   Safety zone to the rear of the barrier to allow travellers to move out of the motorway corridor via an escape door.
This will probably tie in with the maintenance zone.

5.   Planting to help integrate barrier into local surroundings.

6.   Safety fence may be required depending on vertical alignment of barrier and the distance of the barrier from the carriageway.

4.55 Horizontal alignments and land use

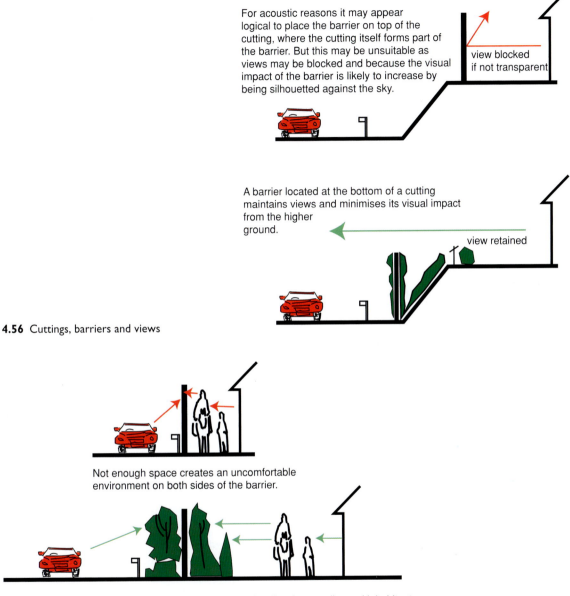

For acoustic reasons it may appear logical to place the barrier on top of the cutting, where the cutting itself forms part of the barrier. But this may be unsuitable as views may be blocked and because the visual impact of the barrier is likely to increase by being silhouetted against the sky.

view blocked if not transparent

A barrier located at the bottom of a cutting maintains views and minimises its visual impact from the higher ground.

view retained

4.56 Cuttings, barriers and views

Not enough space creates an uncomfortable environment on both sides of the barrier.

Additional space removes barrier from personal space leaving the traveller and inhabitants feeling more comfortable and allows the appearance of the barrier to be softened over time through planting.

4.57 Barriers and the need for space

For acoustic reasons, barriers are generally positioned as close as possible to the noise source, so as to be most effective. However, visually this is not desirable as it is preferable in most locations to provide space on both sides of the barrier. These spaces perform a number of visual functions: distance allows the driver/traveller/pedestrian to be separated from the barrier, thus avoiding or reducing a feeling of claustrophobia; distance also reduces the apparent scale of objects; most importantly, space gives the scope for planting, which is a crucial design element. The use of these spaces can conflict with acoustic design objectives and it is necessary to reach a compromise (Figures 4.56 and 4.57).

Setting a road within a cutting is a technique often used to reduce noise. However, additional screening may be required to achieve the noise objective. This would usually involve placing a barrier at the top of the cutting slope, but this could negate the visual benefits provided by the cutting. Furthermore, it can exacerbate the visual impact by silhouetting the barrier against the skyline. This again is an area where a compromise between the acoustic and landscape objectives will need to be reached.

Cost obviously plays a large part in dictating overall design concepts. Once again though, costs should be properly balanced against environmental and visual impacts, and the potential effects on the quality of life. It must be remembered that barriers will be part of the landscape for a long period of time. It is important that these structures and the materials they comprise stand the test of time and they will not do this if the visual quality of the barrier is sacrificed for cost-cutting reasons.

Choosing materials – visual neutrality and compatibility

One way of choosing materials for a barrier on aesthetic grounds is to link the character of the landscape/townscape in a 'neutral' way with the character of the materials. Thus, for example, in rural agricultural areas where the predominant character may comprise the earth itself, grass and native trees and shrubs, it makes sense to integrate the barrier with an earth mound and with grass, trees and shrubs that are visually and materially neutral. Where, for example, a barrier is required to pass through a woodland, it can be appropriate for it to be designed using timber or other organic materials, that are materially and visually sympathetic with the character of the environment. Transparent barriers, which are visually neutral, also tend to be visually effective in rural landscapes.

Alternatively, if the landscape character is dominated by the route corridor itself, with road furniture and buildings clearly visible, the barrier is likely to be much more successful if explicit reference to these is made in the design and in the use of similar manufactured nonorganic materials. An excellent example of where visual neutrality, form, function and aesthetics work hand in hand with the environment, is located along the TGV line into Paris (Figure 4.58). Here the materials chosen tie in with the overall character of the railway line which is dominated by steel in the gantries, cables, railway tracks, etc. The grey–pink colour of the steel barrier is balanced against the background colours of apartment blocks, which are generally pastel shades of pink, ochre and grey. (The combining of materials within a barrier is discussed in Chapter 5.)

The issue of compatibility becomes particularly important and more challenging in situations where more than one barrier is required. These situations occur where barriers are required on either side of a road corridor, when a central reservation barrier is used or where they are aligned between road and rail corridors. It is recommended that materials are co-ordinated

4.58 Well-chosen neutral colours and materials allow a large structure to integrate with its surroundings

4.59 Planting unifies the visual appearance across road and rail corridors

carefully between the barriers and across the routes. This can be achieved by using barriers with similar colours, but often the principal method is to use planting as a unifying theme (Figure 4.59).

Reference

1. OECD (1995) *Roadside noise abatement*, OECD, Paris.

Types of barrier and barrier materials

5

Introduction

There are broadly three types of acoustic barrier, namely reflective, absorptive and reactive which would initially be selected for acoustic reasons, but this choice also determines the range of possible appearances. By their nature, absorptive and reactive barriers are always opaque, whereas reflective noise barriers may be opaque and act as visual barriers as well, or they may be transparent and lighter in appearance. Transparent barriers allow full or partial views through the barrier and light is not obstructed as is the case with an opaque structure. Frosting, colouring, silkscreening and other techniques are used to reduce transparency where views and light may need to be partially obstructed. These barriers also appear lighter in form, but may have the advantage, if required, of partially screening open views to traffic (Figure 5.1).

5.1 Semitransparent noise barrier provides a visual screen while maintaining natural light to a footpath

Typical particle concrete or woodfibre sections

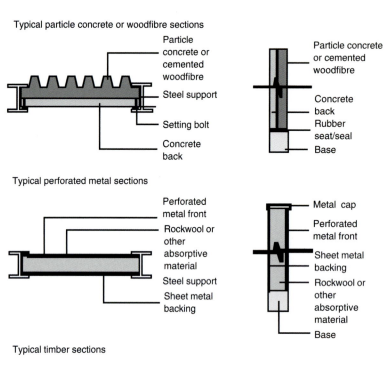

Particle concrete or cemented woodfibre

Steel support

Setting bolt

Concrete back

Particle concrete or cemented woodfibre

Concrete back

Rubber seat/seal

Base

Typical perforated metal sections

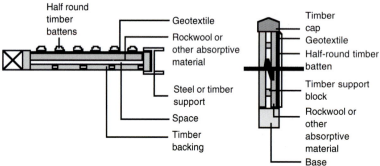

Perforated metal front

Rockwool or other absorptive material

Steel support

Sheet metal backing

Metal cap

Perforated metal front

Sheet metal backing

Rockwool or other absorptive material

Base

Typical timber sections

Half round timber battens

Geotextile

Rockwool or other absorptive material

Steel or timber support

Space

Timber backing

Timber cap

Geotextile

Half-round timber batten

Timber support block

Rockwool or other absorptive material

Base

Typical ceramic/brick sections

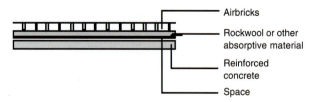

Airbricks

Rockwool or other absorptive material

Reinforced concrete

Space

5.2 Typical absorptive-type barrier sections

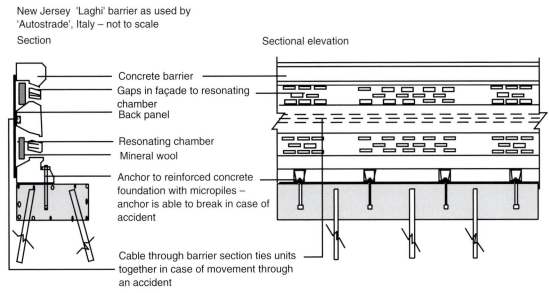

New Jersey 'Laghi' barrier as used by 'Autostrade', Italy – not to scale

Section

Sectional elevation

Concrete barrier

Gaps in façade to resonating chamber

Back panel

Resonating chamber

Mineral wool

Anchor to reinforced concrete foundation with micropiles – anchor is able to break in case of accident

Cable through barrier section ties units together in case of movement through an accident

5.3 New Jersey 'Laghi' barrier with resonators

Sound-absorptive barriers contain a porous element that absorbs noise. This porous material can form the surface of the barrier as is the case with concreted woodfibre and granular concrete barriers. Less robust absorptive materials, such as mineral wool, are protected and enclosed within a skin, where the side facing the noise is perforated. These casings are usually made from timber, steel or aluminium sheeting and brick (Figure 5.2).

Reactive barriers are those which incorporate cavities or resonators designed to attenuate particular frequencies of noise. Sound enters these cavities via small holes or slots in the face of the barrier. Block-work barriers incorporating such cavities have been in use for many years but a recent development has been to incorporate these within a New Jersey safety barrier. This system has been patented and has been installed in the vicinity of Milan (Figure 5.3).

DMRB guidelines

The Highways Agency has published guidance on the use of materials for barriers in its *Design Manual For Roads and Bridges*.[1, 2] This guidance is intended for the design of noise mitigation for trunk roads and motorways but is also relevant to the design of barriers in other locations. Advice is given for a range of materials and, where appropriate, reference is made to the following Highways Agency design specifications and British Standards which should be complied with:

- Timber: *Specification for Highway Works* (MCHW 1) clauses 304, 310 and 311; BS 5268 Part 2, *Structural Use of Timber*.

- Brick walls: *Specification for Highway Works* (MCHW 1) Series 2400; BS 5628 Part 2, *Code of Practice for Use of Masonry*.
- Concrete: *Specification for Highway Works* (MCHW 1) Series 1700 and 2000; BS 8110 Part 1, *Structural Use of Concrete*.
- Metal: BS 5950 Parts 1 and 5, *Structural Use of Steelwork in Building*; BS 8118, *Structural Use of Aluminium*.
- Transparent materials: German standard ZTV Lsw-88.

For each material type, the advice lists many of the qualities and characteristics that can influence the appearance and design of a barrier. Durability is seen as an important factor and all barrier materials are required to remain serviceable for 40 years and require no maintenance for 20 years. Some potential drawbacks associated with each material are also listed, although no advice is given on ways of overcoming such problems. In addition to the range of manufactured materials described, it is also noted that vegetated barrier systems can be used to good effect, but no mention is made that these need regular maintenance.

The guidance given in the *DMRB* is essentially a design checklist and it is clearly drawn both from experience in the UK and overseas. Although containing much useful information, it is not comprehensive. An example of this is found in its discussion of the treatment of transparent materials to deter birds from flying into a barrier. It is noted that materials may be tinted or a pattern of thin opaque stripes may be applied, but no mention is made of other techniques that are in use. In some countries, silhouettes of raptors are often applied to the barriers, but these do not enhance the appearance of the barrier in any way and should be avoided except where they form part of an overall design concept (Figures 5.4 and 5.5). Moreover, tinted glass should primarily be used as a design element and not to deter birds.

When dealing with the need for maintenance, it is noted that transparent barriers require more cleaning than other materials, but this is not necessarily the case if surface treatments are applied which inhibit the settling of dirt and render the barrier self-cleaning in rain. Attention could also be drawn to ingenious solutions which have been adopted to facilitate cleaning. In

5.4 Silkscreened stripes and bold jointing can deter birds and can create successful visual elements

5.5 Deterring birds using bird silhouettes appears naive and diminishes the design integrity of the barrier

5.6 Hinged transparent barrier allows the inaccessible rear to be cleaned

Italy a collapsible transparent barrier has been installed near Milan which incorporates a hinge, allowing the inaccessible rear façade to be lowered and cleaned from the carriageway (Figure 5.6).

The *DMRB* advice on materials highlights many important issues associated with barrier materials and their maintenance. It does not attempt to offer guidance on the selection of materials for particular situations. Barrier designers will need to use the *DMRB* in conjunction with other advice when developing successful barrier concepts.

Noise barrier types

Earth mounds

Earth mounds or bunds are often used to screen development and infrastructure projects. Indeed, earth mounding and the creation of false cuttings are ubiquitously found alongside motorways and trunk roads in rural, semirural and even in urban and suburban locations (see Figure 4.15; Figures 5.7–5.9). In the appropriate location, earth mounds have distinct advantages over other noise barriers in that they:

- may have a natural appearance and may not appear to be noise barriers at all;
- may create an open feeling, in contrast to a vertical or cantilevered screen;
- normally do not require additional safety fences;
- may cost less if excess material is available from construction;
- may be less costly to maintain;
- usually have an unlimited life span.

Earth mounds may be effectively integrated into the local landscape context and, when they are planted or seeded with grass and/or wild flowers, they may form an attractive barrier which will in time be unrecognisable as a barrier

5.7 A well-planted earth mound protects a suburban environment

5.8 An earth mound used as an ornamental feature for a retirement home

5.9 Earth mounds in rural areas can be used for habitat creation and ecological enhancement

in the landscape. Earth mounds do, however, require much more space than a vertical barrier. This is because the earth mound comprises a berm at the top and sloping sides and also generally needs to be higher than a vertical barrier to achieve the same acoustic performance (Figure 5.10). However, it should be noted that space may be needed for planting on each side of a tall vertical barrier to make it visually acceptable.

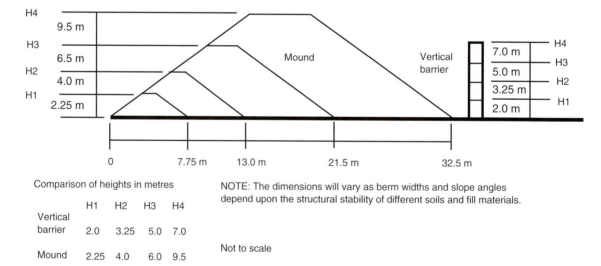

Comparison of heights in metres

	H1	H2	H3	H4
Vertical barrier	2.0	3.25	5.0	7.0
Mound	2.25	4.0	6.0	9.5

NOTE: The dimensions will vary as berm widths and slope angles depend upon the structural stability of different soils and fill materials.

Not to scale

5.10 Mound/vertical barrier height comparison (adapted from Roads and Traffic Authority of NSW[3])

As with any barrier, there are two sides to any mound or bund. The side slopes of either side of the mound may need to be treated differently. The side slopes of the mound are determined by a number of factors:

- the required acoustic performance of the mound;
- the geotechnical nature of the material make-up of the mound;
- the height of the mound relative to its topographical surroundings;
- the cost of the material that will make up the mound;
- the availability of space to accommodate the mound;
- the landscape character of the adjacent land and its land use, also the appropriate angle of repose of the soil to help integrate it into the landscape context.

The severity of the slope may well be determined by the acoustic need to keep the face of the slope as close to the noise source as possible, which will in turn help to keep the mound lower than would be the case if the slope was eased. However, the more extreme the side slopes of a mound, the more difficult it is to construct and plant. In addition, planting would have more difficulty in becoming well established and may require more frequent and costly maintenance. Mounds with severe slopes also tend to look unnatural in the landscape, although in urban-scapes the matter of unnaturalness is less important. It is also worth noting that, from the point of view of road or rail users, the unnaturalness may not be a decisive factor as the route corridors themselves are hardly natural elements in the landscape. The rear side of these mounds and the interface with the natural landscape is, however, different and every effort should be made to integrate the mound as naturally as possible with its surroundings (Figure 5.11).

The appropriation of land is a serious issue and there is pressure to keep mound gradients as steep as possible to minimise land-take. Expert geotechnical advice will be needed to determine the maximum slope that can be achieved to avoid soil slippage for the given soil characteristics and mound height required. In most cases, the maximum side slopes tend to be in the range from 1:2 to 1:3. All planting on slopes will need maintenance and

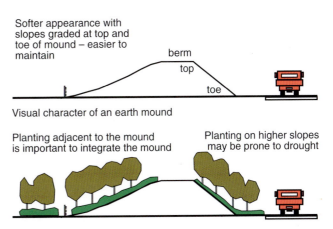

Softer appearance with slopes graded at top and toe of mound – easier to maintain

berm

top

toe

Visual character of an earth mound

Planting adjacent to the mound is important to integrate the mound

Planting on higher slopes may be prone to drought

Planting and an earth mound

5.11 Earth mounds – slopes and planting

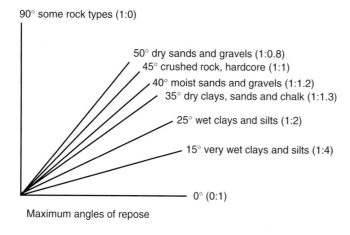

5.12 Soil slope diagram (after the *New Metric Handbook*[4])

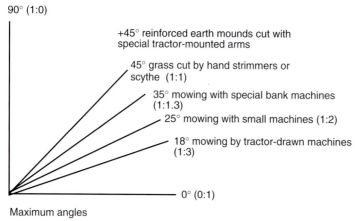

5.13 Soil slope and grass cutting diagram (after the *New Metric Handbook*[4])

the slope angle will determine the way that maintenance is carried out. With shrubs and trees, maintenance is usually carried out less frequently than with grass. Grass slopes can be maintained by mowing (Figures 5.12 and 5.13).

In rural areas, it is usually more appropriate to minimise gradients on pasture land to 1:6 or less to allow grazing. In arable areas, side slopes of 1:10 or less are appropriate to allow for mechanised farming. Where possible, the gradient of the mound should match the natural slope of the surrounding land. In this way, a greater proportion of the land may be returned to its original use. During construction, every attempt should be made to retain the existing soil characteristics, by appropriate soil stripping and storage, and by restoring it with appropriate laying techniques. Care must be taken when importing subsoil and topsoil, that their characteristics are compatible with the existing soils. Notwithstanding, land which is disturbed during construction and returned to agriculture will not necessarily be of the same quality as its surroundings. The resultant disturbance of topsoil and soil structure may adversely affect drainage. For these reasons, not all farmers favour this solution.

Steep profiles may look engineered, especially until planting becomes established that is more difficult on steep slopes than on shallow ones. To reduce the engineered effect, the profile of the mound may be varied along its length as this will help to give it a more natural appearance, which may be particularly important where the surrounding topography is undulating. The merging of the top of the mound into the berm and its toe into the ground also affects its character. In certain situations a clean appearance may be what is required but sharp transitions between horizontal planes and slopes are more difficult to maintain (see Figure 5.11).

When deciding the grading of the mound, it is essential to keep the drainage characteristics of the mound and of the surrounding land in mind. Consideration must also be given to the fact that the upper parts of the mound will tend to be drier as water will move downwards towards the toe of the mound. Planting must then be designed according to this constraint.

Structures with steeper than 1:1 and even 1:0.5 slopes may be achieved by using retaining walls to create earth pockets. Although there are many retaining wall systems available, care should be taken to design a composite structure compatible with the landscape. There are also other earth re-inforcing and retaining systems available which incorporate earth as an integral part of the structure. Some of these, which utilise steel mesh and geotextiles, are now being used more frequently and may achieve near-vertical profiles (Figure 5.14). Structures that incorporate grass-seed beds, or are hydro-seeded post-construction, can quickly provide a grass wall with appropriate rainfall or watering. Once the grass has become established, shrubs and climbers may be planted to create a more organic and less engineered effect.

The efficacy of the planting to withstand drought needs to be assessed. It is important, however, that an appropriate maintenance programme is agreed and budgeted for in the initial contract so that the planting is watered and weeded until it is well established. Subsequently, during periods of drought, further watering may be necessary. Irrigation should be considered as part of

5.14 Well-maintained grass slopes on a steep reinforced earth mound

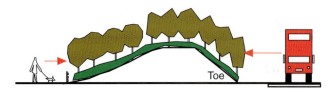

Planting on an earth mound can appear unnatural, as planting may emphasise the mound.

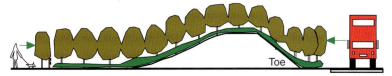

Planting extending beyond the toe of the earth mound helps to disguise the mound.

5.15 Earth mounds – extended planting

the scheme, especially on steep, retained structures, unless the mound is located in a relatively high rainfall area.

Earth mounds and planting

Mounds are planted for a number of reasons. The first is to stabilise the structure by binding soil with root growth, so absorbing water running down the slope. The second is aesthetic, to assimilate it into its landscape context. To integrate it better into the landscape, planting should be considered adjacent to and beyond the toe of the mound. Such planting helps to disguise the profile of a potentially imposing form (Figure 5.15). Mound planting also offers an opportunity to create ecological interest and diversity. With the correct aspect and the right soil and slope gradient, mounds can provide sites for wild flowers and other plant species. Ecological importance is increased if insects, moths and butterflies, invertebrates, small mammals and reptiles are also attracted to the site as a result (see Figure 5.9).

The type of planting relative to aspect and the angle of a slope is an important consideration for mound design, relevant also to cuttings and embankments. Problems occur where rainfall has decreased and where south- to west-facing slopes dry out in the summer sun so that planting and grass struggle to survive. Plant and grass species need to be chosen very carefully. In some areas, where planting may not survive on a slope, a different type of barrier should be used; planting can then be placed at ground level where the roots can take up ground water. An irrigation system would raise the capital cost, but guarantee the long-term success of the design concept.

The second issue that may affect plant growth, survival, character and quality of planting is exposure. Factors such as length of growing season, the temperature range and rainfall influence the choice of plant species. Table 5.1 discusses these influences.[5]

The quality of the design and maintenance of planting is an important factor which affects the visual appearance of a transport corridor. It is generally understood that well-maintained and pristine environments can have a beneficial effect, creating a sense of well-being for both travellers and residents. Poor design and lack of maintenance adversely affect the

Table 5.1 Effects on plants due to slope angles and aspects[5]

The effects of aspect, especially at steep slope angles, significantly modify local climate in two important respects:

- solar radiation input;
- windspeed and direction, in relation to the local prevailing winds.

These in turn affect the local bioclimate at the ground surface and modify:

- the beginning, duration and end of the growing season;
- the potential evapotranspiration and thus soil moisture balance, particularly the intensity of drought;
- the diurnal temperature fluctuations;
- exposure

There are a few empirical studies of some of the effects, but no sufficiently comprehensive models that can be used to predict their likely extent or intensity with respect to the 'normal' data for a horizontal surface. Estimating the effect of local variation of slope is therefore a subjective judgement. Some general guidelines are given below.

Season	Southerly aspects*	Northerly aspects*
Winter	Wide range of diurnal temperature variations with regular freeze–thaw cycles.	Narrow range of diurnal temperatures, stays frozen/cold. Snow cover protects vegetation from exposure.
Spring	Rapid warming of soil, early start to growing season. Early spells with SMD.	Delayed growing season but it is very rare to experience SMD.
Summer	Extreme surface temperatures and very high SMD for extended periods.	Moderate surface temperatures, may avoid prolonged SMDs.
Autumn	Growing season extends into cooler months. SMD takes longer to be reduced by rainfall.	Early end to growing season, early end to SMD.

Season prevailing wind conditions should also be taken into account. The angle of south-facing slope receiving maximum solar radiation input:

Winter	75° from horizontal
Spring/autumn	55° from horizontal
Summer	30° from horizontal

* The effect of other aspects will be intermediate between north and south.
  SMD = soil moisture deficit.

environment and give an appearance of neglect, and ultimately decay. This significantly downgrades the character and quality of the landscape and diminishes the enjoyment of passing travellers. More importantly, it will have a negative effect on the quality of life of local residents. Finally, poor design and maintenance reflect badly on government departments, contractors and design consultants alike.

Timber barriers

Timber barriers have been the most frequently used type of barrier alongside roads in the UK. These tend to resemble garden fence structures and have seldom developed a design identity of their own. Their design, however, has advanced elsewhere in Europe and they deserve to be included in the designer's portfolio. They can fit well into the rural landscape and in some cases they can also appear quite at home in suburban/urban locations; however, they need to be designed beyond the garden fence stage (Figure 5.16). Experience has shown that where barriers are located in residential

5.16 A sympathetically designed timber barrier also serves as a garden boundary

5.17 An urban timber barrier located within a planter provides a more comfortable space for pedestrians and cyclists

5.18 Timber is a totally inappropriate material for a barrier on this concrete overbridge

5.19 The incompatibility of timber and concrete is not reconciled by design elements

areas and close to pedestrian routes, they should be on a human scale so as not to appear imposing or threatening. They should appear as light or as natural as possible without creating dark passages and places where people are wary of walking (Figure 5.17). In Denmark, for example, timber barriers have been used alongside busy urban roads, but recently these have been rejected by local people in favour of lighter barriers, timber or otherwise, which contain appropriate transparent sections. This is because in some areas, where people feel security is an issue, transparent sections make people more visible to one another and thus reduce the chances of attack.

There are, however, locations where timber barriers should be avoided, for example, across viaducts and bridges. The use of the material here, outlined against the sky, is inappropriate and ugly. This is not because it is a poor material or acoustically inadequate, but simply that its rustic character is out of place on concrete or steel. Its organic nature is better suited to being viewed against a backdrop of planting (Figures 5.18 and 5.19). Figure 5.19 shows a well-constructed, interesting timber barrier with variation in the profile, texture and colour, but it looks ill conceived when viewed from the approach to the tunnel. In this location there appears to be no real need to screen views of the traffic and a lighter, more sympathetic transparent material could have been used. The designer must reconcile the intrusive nature of the road and traffic with the potentially incongruous nature of the mitigation. Another situation in which timber should be avoided is where reflective barriers need to be angled for acoustic reasons. Visual expectations dictate that timber fences should be vertical.

Both reflective and absorptive barrier types are available in a wide range of designs. Due to the nature of timber, there is a risk that long stretches of it will be visually boring. Where required for long distances they must be integrated with other barrier types and relieved by planting (Figure 5.20).

5.20 Junction between a timber barrier and a box-type bio-barrier

Although timber barriers are ubiquitous in some parts of Europe, they rarely exceed 4–5 m in height, whereas in the UK they are usually 2–3 m tall. The continental types appear more varied and robust because of their greater scale and the size of the timber slats used; moreover, they look less like garden fences than British ones because the timber slats are often placed horizontally or diagonally and not vertically. The appearance of these barriers is varied according to the kind of wood that is used, and its colour or staining (see Figures 4.43 and 4.13).

The fact that timber is used for domestic fencing means that people have used timber absorptive barriers in domestic situations. These barriers are found mainly along busy suburban routes. They are simply smaller models of the timber barriers found along motorway and rail routes. They are usually constructed with a solid rear face and fronted with an open façade of battens or overlapping slats containing an absorptive internal section of mineral wool (Figures 5.21–5.24). Most timber barriers are supported by steel I-beams, although in some areas these are substituted by concrete or timber posts.

Sheet-metal barriers

Sheet-metal barriers are generally absorptive, but reflective ones have also been made. This type of barrier is usually designed using a perforated metal front façade and a solid steel or aluminium rear panel which is not perforated. Aluminium is often chosen in preference to steel as it is lighter and does not rust. The internal space contains mineral wool or other noise-absorbing materials. The front façade of most of these barriers is profiled to maximise the strength of the panel and thus increase the span widths between posts (Figure 5.25; see also Figure 4.52).

Sheet-metal barriers have been used extensively across Europe, nowhere more so than in Germany, where many have been in place for 15 years or more. The appearance of many of these 4–5 m tall barriers has stood the test of time, mainly because the materials have weathered well, especially where their appearance is not complicated by inept colour and pattern changes. In many cases, their simple metallic surfaces are graded from dark to light and are softened by planting (Figure 5.26). There are many more elaborate barriers of this type, but their location is better suited to the city, where they are assimilated more readily (Figure 5.27). The use of architectonic features is used to good effect in London on the Docklands Light Railway where structural arches support 2 m high vertical and part-cantilevered barriers (Figure 5.28). In future it may be dismissed as a passing fashion but currently it seems that the most visually effective designs are those which respect the integrity of the materials they use. Keeping the lines simple and strong also helps to create a bold, visually coherent solution (Figures 5.29 and 5.30). The simplicity of form and line may be enlivened, however, by using contrasting materials and colours to accent and punctuate the overall design. In Germany, a 4 m high barrier on the A2 by Hanover Hospital includes brick entrance features with cast concrete cornicing, bright-yellow steel support columns and a decorative top rail (see Figures 4.36 and 4.42). These features are continued within an overall design concept which carries through to a bridge across the *autobahn* with a bold yellow façade, and brick and concrete

5.21 (above) A timber absorptive barrier used as a garden fence in a suburban zone

5.22 (opposite) A slatted timber absorptive barrier used in an urban area

5.23 A louvred timber absorptive barrier used as a garden boundary fence

5.24 A substantial timber absorptive motorway barrier with concrete posts and decorative lintels

5.25 Detailed view of a profiled sheet-metal barrier with 6 mm diameter holes

5.26 An older style perforated sheet-metal absorptive barrier graded in tone and softened by planting

5.27 Bold sculptural elements used to add character to an otherwise bland cityscape

5.28 Architectonic features add character to an otherwise plain metal barrier

5.29 Simple lines help to create a bold statement

5.30 Attention to form and respect for materials creates an appropriate visual character for this sheet-metal barrier

5.31 Woodland planting visually isolates the barrier from amenity users

supports. Figure 5.31 shows the rear of the barrier and how planting helps to soften its appearance for people enjoying the adjacent woodland.

Sound-absorbent steel and aluminium panels are often combined with transparent panels as well as other sound-absorptive systems. Figure 5.32 shows such a system on an Italian motorway outside Milan. The aluminium sound-absorptive panels are placed above a sound-absorptive New Jersey 'Laghi' barrier, with stepped transparent windows. Sound-absorbent aluminium/steel panels are also suited for placement on retaining walls, retained cuttings and tunnel entrances, where they can form part of an overall design concept (Figure 5.33).

Many of the same design principles apply to reflective sheet-metal barriers. One of the most extensive and visually successful barriers is the 5 m high aluminium barrier on the A10 Ring around Amsterdam. This imposing barrier, with a profile that echoes an aircraft wing, is a major architectural structure. Its flowing lines, which follow the curvilinear road layout, give a

5.32 Aluminium absorptive panels with transparent windows placed on top of a New Jersey 'Laghi' barrier

5.33 Perforated sheet-metal barrier used at a tunnel entrance

5.34 A free-flowing functional design in aluminium

5.35 Climbing frames and horizontal windows add visual complexity to the smooth, even surface

feeling of dynamism: this high-tech contemporary-looking barrier is a fitting feature on a major route around the city (Figures 5.34 and 5.35). The concept, which hinges on maintaining a seamless, flowing appearance, is further enhanced by narrow, elongated, horizontal windows which are simply used to add interest to a potentially bland, even surface. In total contrast to this, giant climbing frames for planting have been added, which break up the horizontal emphasis and create staccato focal points.

The wing concept again has been taken as an inspiration for a recent construction on the A20 in Rotterdam. Here, a strikingly free-flowing design with concealed supports echoes the aesthetic of a dynamic traffic corridor with curvilinear aluminium panels and acrylic windows. The support structure is an elegant wishbone design. Once again, the transport corridor has been seen to present an opportunity for a good functional and aesthetic design that reflects the environment and the age in which we live (Figure 5.36; see also Figure 4.14). The unusual use of transparent sections for the lower part of a barrier is successful because it reveals a light and sophisticated support structure.

5.36 A well-conceived and implemented architectonic design can improve the motorway setting

Concrete barriers

Like sheet-metal barriers, concrete barriers can be classified according to those which reflect noise and those which absorb noise.

Reflective concrete barriers

Reflective concrete panels and *in situ* concrete constructions can be used as effectively as any other barrier if the overall design is well-conceived, the proportions are correct and where planting is used to create an organic, contrasting texture to the concrete. Flat areas of dull concrete should be avoided by using texturing and robustly patterned form-work to create shifting patterns of light and shade (Figure 5.37; see also Figure 4.40). Texture and interesting finishes may also be achieved through bush-hammering (Figure 5.38). Massive concrete work without some kind of planting or variation in design should be avoided: compare the massive, visually un-accommodating structure in Figure 5.39 with the examples shown in Figures 5.40 and 5.41. These photographs show how the appearance of barriers is dramatically improved by an interesting design coupled with planting. The Virginia creeper is planted in an area of soil less than 300 mm wide.

Concrete blocks have also been used to construct noise barriers, an example of which can be found approaching Tel Aviv (Figure 5.42). Here the colour of the blocks and the pattern tie in with the stone building-block style of construction in Israel; moreover, the rough-textured arrangement of blocks helps to break up a potentially imposing façade.

Most concrete barriers utilise steel I-column posts set within or bolted on concrete foundations. There is, however, one system which requires less extensive footings, by relying on its horizontal alignment to give it structural stability. This system utilises panels which are fanned or snaked and may be constructed up to 10 m or more in height. A greater width is required for the trapezoidal layout but this may be used for planting (Figure 5.43). These barriers may be reflective or absorptive.

5.37 The visual appearance of concrete can be improved by strong patterning and by softening through planting

5.38 A bush-hammered profiled concrete surface provides textural interest and changes in visual quality with the play of light and shade

5.39 A large area of concrete creates an unsightly barrier

5.40 The visual character of a concrete barrier is relieved by design elements and vegetation

5.41 Virginia creeper (*Parthenocissus quinquefolia*) used to completely obscure a concrete barrier

5.42 A concrete-block barrier echoes the vernacular style of the Middle East

5.43 An 11 m high pre-cast concrete articulated barrier

Absorptive concrete barriers

There are basically two types of absorptive concrete barriers, that may be categorised as woodfibre concrete barriers and granular concrete barriers. Both types usually comprise panels made up to size and colour in a factory and are installed between steel supports. The material comprises an open-structured concrete in which either wood fibres or small cementaceous balls are used as the aggregate. The panels are 4–5 m long and usually 140–190 mm thick, depending on whether they are absorptive on one or both sides. Approximately two-thirds of the width of the single-sided panel is absorptive, whereas the rear third comprises solid concrete. The absorptive surface is usually quite highly profiled in order to increase the surface area of the façade and thus maximise the noise absorption. These profiles can be arranged vertically as well as horizontally, or in various patterns, using form-work in the factory (Figures 5.44 and 5.45). Colour may be incorporated into the panels during manufacture by mixing pigments with the concrete mixtures. When viewed from a distance or from a moving vehicle it is difficult to identify which of these two types of absorptive concrete has been used.

Traditionally, woodfibre concrete and granular concrete barriers have been supported by steel or concrete I-columns. Most frequently, the I-columns incorporate a bottom flange which is then bolted onto a steel pile or a concrete footing (Figure 5.46). The panels are placed on concrete footings cast between the column foundations; this ensures that all the panels are perfectly aligned on the same level (Figure 5.47). Joints are normally sealed with compressible rubber strips. The barriers can also be manufactured as complete units which are self-supporting and which can be bolted together to form an apparently seamless barrier.

Brick barriers

Bricks are often used to construct masonry barriers as they fit in with vernacular architecture. Solid bricks are used to construct reflective barriers whereas perforated bricks are used for sound-absorptive barriers: either solution generally creates the impression of a conventional brick wall. These materials can also be used as decorative and functional facings on retaining walls in cuttings. Concrete blocks with perforations can also be used but these present a more engineered and sterile image (see Figures 4.36, 4.42 and 4.43).

5.44 A profiled woodfibre concrete barrier

5.45 A profiled granular concrete barrier
with tree-shaped acrylic windows

5.46 Steel I-column with flange bolted to bolts set into a concrete footing

5.47 Precast panels set between steel posts and set onto *in situ* concrete footings

Plastic, PVC and fibreglass barriers

There are a few examples of barriers that incorporate elements and panels largely composed of plastics, PVC and fibreglass. As plastic recycling increases and these materials become more competitively priced, versatile and robust, it is likely that they will be more widely used. Plastic for many people evokes robust colours and inventive moulded shapes; in this respect, one Parisian barrier exploits the potential of this material with a 5 m high barrier incorporating a series of flowing, brightly coloured moulded tubes attached to acrylic panels (Figure 5.48). However, plastic barriers need not appear so eccentric for they can be moulded to imitate the character of other materials. For example, the 3 m high barrier at Nyborg, in southern Denmark, is made from PVC and yet it appears to look like aluminium or coated steel (Figure 5.49; see also Figure 4.39). The barrier is designed with acrylic windows perpendicular to the PVC panels to allow some views out from the motorway.

Transparent barriers

Transparent noise barriers are constructed from laminated, toughened or reinforced glass or from acrylic or polycarbonate sheet although it is very difficult to differentiate between these materials from a distance. Sheet thicknesses are usually 8–19 mm for glass and 15–20 mm for acrylic and polycarbonate. Sheet sizes vary according to the manufacturer, but acrylic sheet can be cut and worked on site whereas glass usually cannot. Very large sheets of acrylic have been used, up to 9 m in height.

Acrylic sheet can be curved to add stiffness to the panel, thus maximising span widths between posts and avoiding the use of top rails. This helps to maintain a lightness of form, thereby reducing the apparent height of the barrier. Glass barriers, too, can be bent by angling sheets relative to one another to achieve the desired barrier profile. Acrylic sheet can be highly coloured and glass can be subtly tinted and etched (Figures 5.50 and 5.51).

5.48 An older but flamboyant fibreglass barrier

5.49 A clean-looking PVC barrier, but staggering allows views from the motorway into a private garden (see Figure 4.39)

Glass and acrylic sheet are materials which, because of their visual neutrality, have very little impact on the character of the landscape and may be used in most locations where the visual intrusion of traffic is not an overriding issue. Both types of transparent materials are well used across Europe. New planar glazing and curtain walling methods have made it possible to create barriers that are visually high-tech (see Figure 4.35). Transparent barriers have also been constructed using glass block units (Figure 5.52).

Two additional factors that influence the choice between glass or acrylic sheet are resistance to vandalism and transparency. Should vandals try to damage a transparent sheet, glass is more easily broken but acrylic sheet is more readily scratched. Where a totally undistorted view through the barrier is required, toughened glass may be preferred to other transparent materials because these may occasionally give rise to minor distortions. Both materials provide transmissibility of light, although historically glass was preferred where light transmissibility over the lifetime of the barrier was important.

5.50 A functional and aesthetic use of acrylic sheet

5.51 Glass sheets angled to form a cantilevered barrier

5.52 A unique glass block barrier

However, problems of opacity have been overcome with modern acrylics and these now may be guaranteed to maintain their light transmissibility for 10 years. A balance must be struck between these factors when selecting the appropriate transparent material.

In most instances transparent panels have been designed for bridges or viaducts, because their lightweight appearance can be better integrated into the engineering design than opaque panels (Figure 5.53). Transparent barriers also have advantages in other locations because they:

- allow access to views, offering no visual obstruction or sense of claustrophobia;
- allow light to penetrate, retaining natural light conditions behind the barrier;
- are generally neutral and visually less intrusive.

Where a barrier is to be placed in an elevated position above a route corridor it makes sense for it to be transparent to maintain views across and beyond the transport corridor (Figure 5.54). This has the added advantage of reducing the visual impact for drivers. Transparent barriers are not, however, always transparent as they are affected by weather and temperature changes. A 'transparent' barrier in the morning may well be semiopaque until the heat of the day dries off the dew (Figure 5.55).

Where there is close public access to a barrier, it is extremely important to maintain light and a feeling of openness, especially where there is little space available. Figure 5.56 shows a unique 3.5 m high glazed barrier on the Bern Ostring (East Ring Road) located immediately adjacent to apartment buildings and a public footpath. Adequate noise attenuation is cleverly balanced with the provision of space and light: closely spaced vertical aluminium sound-absorptive fins are placed at 90° to the front face and a plain, glazed profile to the rear (Figure 5.57).

5.53 (opposite) An overall confident and well-engineered design includes the barrier within the overall design concept

5.54 A transparent barrier allows views above and beyond the traffic corridor

5.55 A transparent barrier made nontransparent by morning dew

5.56 A transparent barrier maintains light for a pedestrian footpath

Another problem for the designer in urban locations is that the design must take account not only of the appearance of the barrier from a distance, but also close to: for example, from pedestrian walkways adjacent to the barrier. A barrier may have good lines, shape and form, but to pass close scrutiny it must have sufficient detail and patterning to make it visually interesting. A good example of effective use of shadow to create pattern can be found on a barrier in Copenhagen. As light passes through the silk-screened patterns, the patterns themselves become more intense or diffuse and the shadows cast vary in angle and intensity. The robust, triangular post shape gives a necessary visual gravity to the barrier, but its stocky appearance is broken up by the shadow patterns falling across the posts (see Figures 4.12 and 4.53).

The visual character of the supports is important for all barriers, but it can be particularly so with transparent barriers as they will be more noticeable in

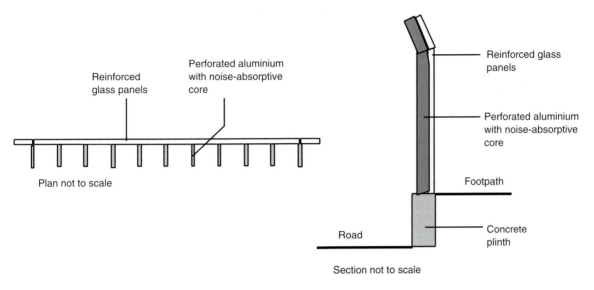

Reinforced glass panels

Perforated aluminium with noise-absorptive core

Plan not to scale

Reinforced glass panels

Perforated aluminium with noise-absorptive core

Footpath

Road

Concrete plinth

Section not to scale

5.57 Reinforced glass and perforated aluminium barrier

5.58 Viewed close up, I-beams have a heavy appearance

relation to the glass panels. In many cases, as with other barriers, steel I-columns are used (Figure 5.58). This profile adds necessary weight to the visual character of the barrier but also appears crude and heavy. A lightness of appearance can be achieved by tapering the posts, and by angling them to create more space and air at the top of the barrier (see Figure 5.4). This lightness of appearance is further enhanced if no rail is used at the top edge of the transparent panel.

Another example where a barrier improves the environmental appearance of a route corridor may be found on the A27 at Gorinchem, Holland. These

5.59 A retrofitted barrier provides noise mitigation and visually enhances an old viaduct

V-shaped concrete barrier support structures improve the visual quality of the viaduct elevation visible to the neighbouring housing areas, footpaths and cycle-ways. The repetitive use of blue-coloured acrylic panels placed within and above the V creates rhythmic, jewel-like focal points along the viaduct, lifting and strengthening the visual impact of the barrier (Figure 5.59). A further well-documented example of where coloured acrylic sheet has been used to good effect is in the 20 m high barriers which protect a series of apartment blocks abutting the Périphérique in Paris (see Figure 1.1). This barrier utilises an innovative space-frame support structure and arrangement of transparent and coloured panels.

In most cases transparent sections are used above other panels to lighten the appearance of the top of the barrier and to reduce its apparent height. In some cases, however, transparent sections may be used as an element in a composite structure whereby the whole appearance of the barrier is lightened. This may be seen in a 3.2 m high barrier on Route 21, west of Copenhagen, Denmark, where glass and sound-absorptive steel panels are sequentially juxtaposed. The steel panels absorb direct sound and sound reflected onto them from the inclined glass panels. At the same time the barrier maintains an open appearance for motorists and allows the properties to the rear of the barrier access to views and light (Figure 5.60).

5.60 The clever juxtaposition of materials provides both sound-absorptive and transparent qualities

Cantilevered barriers

A cantilevered barrier is one which cantilevers out towards and above the noise source. As discussed elsewhere in the book, they may have a number of visual advantages over and above a simple vertical barrier, as follows:

- reducing overall barrier height by locating the top edge of the barrier closer to the noise source, thereby reducing impact;
- diminishing the impact on the viewer from outside the transport corridor because the top part curves away from the viewer and thus appears lighter (see Figure 4.20);
- offering opportunities for bolder, more distinctive design solutions in locations where a boundary fence or wall might appear out of place;
- cantilevering across the carriageway to form a partial tunnel allows the space above to be used for other purposes.

Cantilevered barriers may be constructed from a range of materials and may vary considerably in height and size. They may be either reflective or sound-absorptive. In Denmark, for example, the railway authority uses a comparatively low-key 2.5–3 m high steel barrier in all locations where noise abatement is required. Although the appearance of the barrier ties in with the utilitarian environment of a railway corridor, it is nevertheless rather dull and uninteresting (Figure 5.61).

At the other end of the scale there are large-scale barriers that are considerable architectural and engineering structures in their own right. The long, 10 m high concrete cantilevered barrier on the A28 at Zeist, the Netherlands, for example, protects a large estate of high-rise apartments. On the road side, the barrier boldly cantilevers out over the hard shoulder, whereas on the side of the development, robust buttressing counterbalances

5.61 A simple small-scale cantilevered railway barrier

the ascending cantilevered roof (see Figures 2.2 and 2.3). When viewed from the road, the success of this barrier may be attributed to the profile of the roof which arcs smoothly against the sky as it follows the curved alignment of the road. The end profiles are of two different designs: at one end, the façade is angled skywards, giving the profile a dynamic, floating appearance, whereas the other end is staggered in a series of giant steps. Existing woodland has been left untouched between the road and the buildings. The resulting distance between the apartments and the barrier diminishes the impact of such an imposing structure and it is further softened by the retained mature trees. The ordered megalithic concrete buttresses complement the design and echo the pattern of the tree trunks.

Another barrier built on a similar scale was recently completed on the A16 at Dordrecht, Holland. This 9 m tall construction screens a complex of older style apartment blocks and their public spaces from increasing traffic noise levels. The transparent cantilever extends beyond the hard shoulder, supported by a series of prestressed arched concrete columns and a steel lattice frame. The elements comprise dark-coloured profiled concrete panels with intermittent transparent panels at the lower levels. The upper levels are fully transparent. The confident high-tech design, featuring details such as

5.62 A well-conceived contemporary design allows a large structure to be acceptable in the landscape

5.63 Interesting variations in form create a high-tech contemporary image

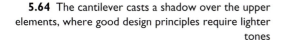

5.64 The cantilever casts a shadow over the upper elements, where good design principles require lighter tones

signage structures which curve towards the barrier and echo its shape, signals a resolve to address the increasing noise problems in a fearlessly creative way, entirely in keeping with the urban location (Figures 5.62 and 5.63).

Another massive structure which is not, however, as visually appealing, is the 6 m high sound-absorbent barrier on the A3 at Neudorf, near Duisberg, Germany. This barrier, too, is supported by prestressed concrete columns, but is heavier in appearance, being constructed of granular concrete. Trees behind the barrier help to soften the top profile, but the aspect from the road will inevitably be 'hard' since there is little room for planting; moreover, planting would be difficult to establish and maintain on the front face, or adjacent to it, without irrigation. The choice of the robust Roman copper colour, used successfully elsewhere across Europe, suggests that there has been little attempt to disguise this barrier and initially it appears rather heavy. The problem with the choice of a single colour here is that the cantilever shades the upper portion of the barrier so that the very part that should be lighter in tone appears darker. However, in this situation a transparent section could not be used because of the need to provide sound absorption (Figure 5.64).

The 6 m high perforated aluminium absorptive barrier located on the N2 near Bellinzona in southern Switzerland offers a better visual solution to the problem of providing substantial sound-absorbing cantilevered barriers. Twin cantilevered barriers on either side of the southbound carriageway and a high-tech appearance do not conflict with the semirural, picturesque landscape of the Swiss mountains and lakes. The clean lines of the elegant form wind around the mountain topography to good effect, a model of good design and precise engineering. Although initially surprising, this effect is acceptable in the landscape. Other materials may have been suitable, for example glass or acrylic, but they would not have provided the required sound absorption. The designers succeeded by applying the principle of using a high-quality design in a high-quality landscape. Planting is used systematically at the front and rear of the barrier, which helps to soften the bottom edges. In fact, the whole design is well-conceived, the landscape and road layout outside the barrier forming part of a greater design concept (Figures 5.65 and 5.66; see also Figure 4.23).

5.65 A well-designed high-tech solution fits in well even in scenic areas

5.66 The use of space, planting and the alignment allows the aluminium barrier to fit into the landscape

5.67 Thatch barriers can fit in well in rural areas

Thatch barriers

Thatch seems an unlikely material for a noise barrier, yet panels have been used in the Netherlands. The neutral nature of the material allows them to fit well in the rural landscape, especially where there is a vegetative backdrop. Thatch is fire-proofed and placed on a timber panel, supported by steel I-columns and topped with a timber or ceramic cap (Figure 5.67). Frames or wires can be attached to allow climbing plants to create a more organic and natural appearance. Relief patterns can be cut into the thatch, as they are on thatched roofs in rural England.

Bio-barriers

Bio-barriers are structures that incorporate planting as an integral part of their design. They are being researched and developed across Europe, particularly in the Netherlands. Some early bio-barriers proved unsatisfactory for a number of reasons, such as the need for maintenance and irrigation, but newer designs have addressed these problems. In the UK, however, there is continuing resistance to bio-barriers precisely because of these early teething troubles and the need for continued maintenance (Figures 5.68 and 5.69).

The question of irrigation and maintenance raises fundamental concerns about attitudes towards barrier provision. Where the decision has been made to provide a barrier to meet legal or design objectives, the appropriate barrier should be chosen and the concomitant maintenance must be regarded as an essential part of the scheme. The need for periodic maintenance should not inhibit this choice.

A range of natural-looking bio-barriers has been developed which offers an alternative to earth mounds. These have the advantage that they do not require the space needed for a mound, in effect creating a living barrier on a narrow strip of land (Figure 5.70). As well as reducing land-take, these bio-barriers act as wildlife corridors creating habitats for small mammals and insects.

Experience has shown that the successful appearance of a bio-barrier depends on:

- compatibility of plant species with soil conditions and type (soils must be analysed for fertility, acidity, salinity, contaminants, organic content and drainage);
- density of planting (plants should not compete with one another);
- provision of irrigation or watering during plant establishment;
- provision of irrigation and watering through dry periods;
- establishment of an appropriate plant maintenance regime, including weed control, pruning, application of fertilisers and replacement of dead plants.

For ease of categorisation, bio-barriers may be divided into four generic types, the names of which reflect the main structures or principles of the design:

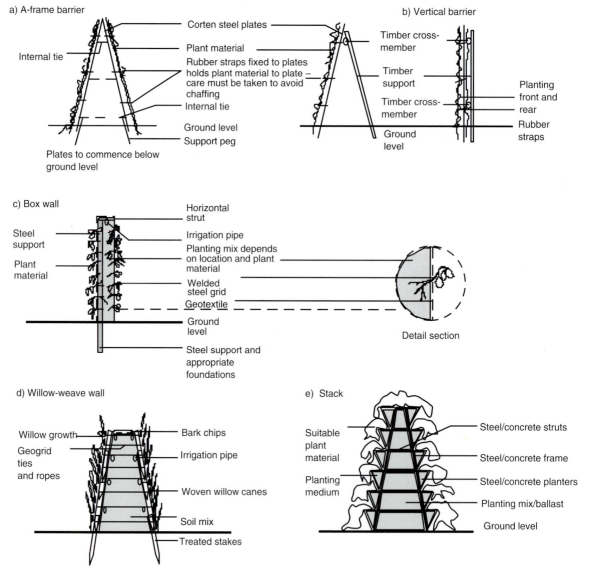

5.68 Bio-barrier sections

- A-frame and vertical corten steel bio-barriers;
- box wall bio-barriers;
- woven-willow bio-barriers;
- stack and crib bio-barriers.

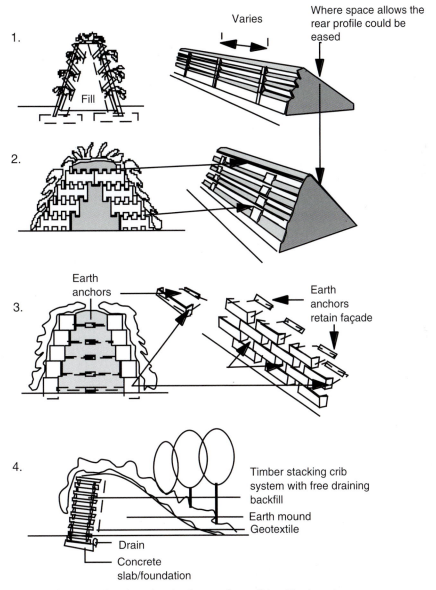

Interlocking systems utilising concrete/timber panels and supports with earth planting pockets

1.

Varies

Where space allows the rear profile could be eased

Fill

2.

3.

Earth anchors

Earth anchors retain façade

4.

Timber stacking crib system with free draining backfill

Earth mound
Geotextile

Drain

Concrete slab/foundation

Note: In many situations the planting medium will tend to dry out when there is little rainfall. Supplementary irrigation may then be required.

5.69 Crib and stacking systems

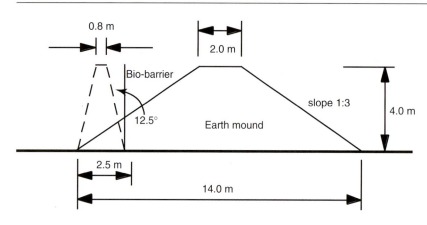

5.70 Comparative land-take for a 4 m high earth mound and a 4 m high bio-barrier

0.8 m

2.0 m

Bio-barrier

12.5°

slope 1:3

Earth mound

4.0 m

2.5 m

14.0 m

A-frame and vertical corten steel bio-barriers

The A-frame barrier consists of two slightly corrugated corten steel sheets which are splayed at the base, anchored to the ground with treated timber staves and angled to form an apex. The corten steel, which forms an anticorrosive rust on the surface to protect the inner core of the steel, acts as a reflective barrier and is expected to have a useful life of more than 20 years. Plant material is placed immediately adjacent to both sides of the barrier at regular intervals and trained up it using loose rubber ties. Care is taken that the plants do not scrape or chafe against the plates in the wind. Before the planting is established, and during the winter where deciduous planting is used, the steel plates give the barrier a rust colour. This natural colour blends easily into rural/semirural areas. In summer and once the planting is established, the steel is mostly screened and the barrier gives the appearance of a dense, tapering hedge (Figure 5.71 and see Figure 5.68(a)). Thus, deciduous planting allows the appearance of the barrier to change colour according to the season, in keeping with its surroundings. Planting can be varied according to the location and species such as willow, alder, ash, field maple, privet, lime and ivy have been used in the Netherlands.

The vertical corten steel barrier comprises a single sheet of corrugated corten steel which may be placed vertically or splayed slightly. The steel

5.71 A-frame barrier with alder

plates are supported by a timber frame to the rear. Planting is usually placed on both sides of the barrier, screening the steel sheets on the front and the frame to the rear. Care should be taken to provide a stable structure as any movement disturbs the plants' roots and inhibits growth (see Figure 5.68(b)). Both A-frame and vertical barriers are installed by Mostert and De Winter in the Netherlands and are registered as 'Geluid Groeischerm' (Sound-proofing Growing Screen).

In the Netherlands, willow, the most commonly used species with this type of barrier, provides a suitable biotope for some insects. The suitability of willow species, however, should be assessed according to the ground conditions. In areas of low rainfall, irrigation may be needed. Some willows, too, may be sensitive to salt spray and salt in the ground, and susceptible to some diseases and pests, especially in the initial stages of growth. The issue of spray from roads that have been de-iced using salt and the resulting accumulation of salt in the soil is an important consideration for all roadside and barrier planting.

Finally, although these barriers are welcome additions to the designers' portfolio, they are relative newcomers only and there are still a few problems associated with structures, fixings, the long-term establishment of some planting, and damage to plants in high winds and other extreme weather conditions. Close planting is not an option since subjects fail due to root competition. Maintenance of the planting and its fixings is an issue complicated by the choice of plant species, the need to train or prune some subjects and to maintain the form of the original design.

Box wall bio-barriers

The box wall bio-barrier comprises an earth wall within a steel mesh frame with supports. Inside this, the soil mix is contained in a geotextile or polyethylene sheet. The soil mix is adjusted to suit the plant types used. Planting is introduced at intervals in the vertical sides of the wall through the

5.72 Green box bio-barrier along a suburban route in the Netherlands

steel mesh, in holes cut into the geotextile or polyethylene (Figure 5.72). The barrier may be constructed to more than 6 m high, although most existing box wall bio-barriers are 2–4 m high. As the barrier is only approximately 0.6 m wide, it may dry out; therefore irrigation is necessary. Most barriers in the Netherlands are planted with ivy (*Hedera helix*), which usually grows to completely cover the underlying structure, thus creating an attractive green wall. Their narrow profile and organic but tidy appearance fit into urban, suburban and rural areas (see Figure 5.68(c)). They also tie in well with other barriers (see Figure 5.20). Soil-less box wall barriers are available that utilise a mineral wool core in which the plants are established. The mineral wool material absorbs moisture from the ground which passes through the barrier by capillary action; however, although moisture is held within the barrier by capillary breaks, it is advisable to install a dual-purpose irrigation/fertilisation system. In all box systems, planting can be established at the toe of the wall and trained to climb up it. If UV-sensitive polyethylene soil containment sheets are used, vigorous root growth is essential to bind the soil as the sheet deteriorates. This problem is avoided if a geotextile is used which is not UV-sensitive and has a longer life-span.

Willow-weave bio-barriers

Woven willow barriers are a patented Dutch invention incorporating vertical staves through which willow whips are woven to form a large cane basket filled with soil, or an appropriate mix. The construction is reinforced using staves, ties and ropes (see Figure 5.68(d)). Irrigation pipes can be included within the construction. Willow tends to grow quickly, about 2 m each season. These whips must be trimmed during the dormant season. Willow walls can create an effective screen, but care must be taken that the construction is sufficiently robust. Experience in the Netherlands has demonstrated that many of the horizontal willow whips do not take root and so give the structure no extra stability. However, British installers of these

5.73 A woven-willow barrier awaiting pruning in winter

barriers claim that additional supports and more durable ties have overcome these stability problems (Figure 5.73).

Stack bio-barriers

The stack barrier is literally a wall of precast units stacked one on top of the other. Most start wider at the base and as the wall steps upwards the number of units in each layer is decreased. In the past, barriers were constructed using precast concrete pipe units containing ballast and earth in which planting could be established. These developed into a number of different kinds of stackable earth-retaining systems. The overall appearance of the these barriers depends on the character and maintenance of the planting (Figures 5.74 and 5.75).

5.74 A vertical stacked concrete pipe barrier well-integrated into a domestic setting with planting

5.75 A concrete stack barrier with planting pockets

5.76 A stack barrier using coated steel pockets fixed to a steel frame

5.77 A fully vegetated concrete crib system provides a large verdant screen

A steel stack system has also been developed. This incorporates a galvanised steel frame on which lightweight earth-filled coated-steel pockets are suspended. These pockets are planted with appropriate plant species. An irrigation system may be required. The base of the unit is approximately 1.6 m wide for a height of 5 m. The barrier faces are angled at 10° from the vertical (Figure 5.76 and see Figure 5.68).

Crib wall bio-barriers

Although concrete and timber crib systems are mainly used for earth retention, they can be used as noise barriers by incorporating the cribs on both sides or by using the crib face to steepen the front face of an earth bund. Timber cribs are usually back-filled with a free-draining rock while some pockets are filled with earth and are planted. Most often, however, where planting is required, it is located at the top and encouraged to cascade down. With concrete cribs, soil is usually placed in the pockets to support planting and irrigation is important to help maintain the planting in good order (Figure 5.77 and see Figure 5.69).

Integrated barriers

The term integrated barrier is used to identify those barriers which are integrated into the local fabric as utilitarian features. Thus, the first function of the barrier may be a garage, or a storeroom, or a factory unit, while the design and location of the form allows it to also act as a noise barrier. This kind of mitigation is becoming increasingly prevalent in Europe, where new development is proposed alongside busy traffic corridors. In an example at De Lied in the Netherlands, the houses closest to the main road have been provided with a storeroom and open storage area with a large rear wall and sloping roof. These structures are placed in a line at the far end of the gardens

5.78 A continuous row of storerooms facing the road protects the adjacent homes and gardens

5.79 Podium block containing car park and shopping areas provides screening for residential tower blocks

facing onto the road. This means that both the gardens and the houses are protected from traffic noise while providing necessary household storage facilities (Figure 5.78). A larger-scale example of this type of barrier may be found in Hong Kong where podium blocks containing car parks and commercial areas are commonly constructed to protect large multistorey housing blocks (Figure 5.79).

A stunning example on the N3 in Dordrecht, the Netherlands, illustrates a fully developed environmental approach to designing a new housing development adjacent to an elevated trunk road. The designers of this large development have used two methods to mitigate noise. The first has been the construction of large 9 m high transparent barriers which enclose the housing area and which, in one part, are attached to the housing to provide sheltered courtyards and conservatories. This is an architecturally dynamic form that reduces noise and provides a sheltered place to sit, while maintaining views to the lake beyond. Doors in the barrier are provided to allow access to the lake (Figures 5.80 and 5.81). The environmental design is taken further by locating part of the development in a large man-made bund that faces the road. This large earth structure provides insulation for these houses and noise protection for the rest of the development.

Barrier materials on bridges

Barriers located on viaducts and bridges should, from a visual aesthetic point of view, be kept as light and as simple as possible, but they should also reflect the surrounding landscape character. Where visual intrusion of vehicles is not a significant issue, transparent or part-transparent barriers should be used.

The design detail of a noise barrier across a bridge or viaduct should harmonise with the base structure. On bridges, where space is at a premium, noise barriers must be located close to the safety barriers. This can result in visual clutter. The increasing use of concrete parapets as safety barriers avoids this as noise barriers can be mounted on them, achieving a cleaner, simpler appearance (Figure 5.82).

5.80 A glass and steel barrier and a large earth mound with internal housing provides noise protection as part of an overall environmental strategy for a large housing project

5.81 Close-up view of the 9 m high glass barrier that protects the housing behind

5.82 Mounting the noise barrier on top of a concrete safety fence avoids visual clutter

5.83 Planting on a bridge structure can link the structure into the surrounding landscape

5.84 Formal planting on a bridge in an urban environment helps to soften the cityscape

Barrier panels should be tied together and to the structure so that they cannot be easily dislodged if hit by a vehicle (see Figure 6.1).

Planting on viaducts and bridges is possible and can be used to create an effective visual screen and may also improve the visual character of the structure within its context. Although no examples of this technique are known, noise barriers with integrated planters should be considered, especially if the viaduct extends from one planted area to another (Figures 5.83 and 5.84).

Barriers and solar panels

The introduction of solar panels on noise barriers is at an experimental stage. Such barriers have been built in several countries. At present, however, generation of solar power is far more costly than conventional electricity generation, but it is feasible that these costs will drop significantly over time

5.85 Solar panels designed as part of an overall concept

as technology improves. Apart from the costs, using noise barriers for a secondary purpose is a good idea. However, the barriers must be located where they cannot be damaged by vandals and the solar cells should be designed as an integral part of the barrier, not just an add-on (Figure 5.85; see also Figure 4.10). In more urban areas it is possible that the generated electricity could be used to light up a feature or the barrier itself, creating a contemporary sculptural element.

Tunnels

Placing a transport corridor in a tunnel offers the most effective visual and acoustic solution, but it is invariably the most expensive. However, where cut and cover tunnelling is used the land above can be used for amenity or development purposes thus defraying the capital cost (Figures 5.86 and 5.87(a); see also Figure 5.33). The photographs and diagram show the tunnel portal with a perforated aluminium absorptive central reserve barrier at the approach. The covered area has been reclaimed from the traffic corridor to be

5.86 Public open space provided above a motorway hidden below within a cut and cover tunnel

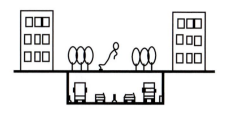

(a) Cut and cover tunnel

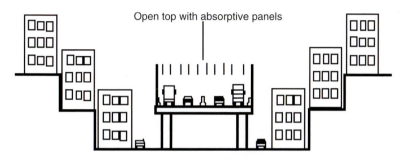

Open top with absorptive panels

(b) Tunnel on viaduct with absorptive roof baffles

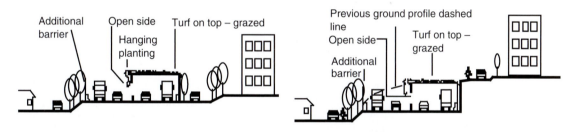

Additional barrier | Open side | Hanging planting | Turf on top – grazed

Previous ground profile dashed line
Open side
Turf on top – grazed
Additional barrier

(c) Open sided gallery above ground level

(d) Open sided gallery contained within the landform

5.87 Tunnels

used as an urban park. Nevertheless, tunnels do not always need to be below ground, nor do they need to be fully enclosed.

A grand example of a tunnel above ground is to found in the centre of Genoa, Italy (Figure 5.87(b)). The conditions here are extreme and design options limited: the area is densely developed on rising ground, with multistorey apartment blocks located within metres of a viaduct built by Mussolini in the 1930s. Because of the high volume of traffic the viaduct is now topped with a 270 m long and 6 m high, partially open-roofed tunnel. This comprises a louvred cover of vertical acoustic panels which allows light into the tunnel, lets exhaust gases escape and attenuates noise from the traffic. The tunnel sides comprise sound-absorptive panels above a concrete New Jersey barrier. The construction is lightweight and is fixed using steel I-columns, steel rods and cables. Autostrade, the organisation responsible for this motorway, reports that local people are happy with the barrier, but that people in apartments level with the barrier have complained about their loss of light (Figures 5.88–5.90).

5.88 Approaching the elevated Genoese tunnel

5.89 Inside the Genoese tunnel which contains absorptive roof and side panels

5.90 The tunnel, which was constructed on an existing viaduct, protects many local residents

An example of a partial or galleried tunnel is located on the N2 motorway near Lucerne, Switzerland. This long open-sided tunnel, which covers one half of the motorway, is cut into a hillside. At the start the reinforced concrete tunnel stands proud above ground level, but the side walls are well concealed with climbers and shrub and tree planting (see Figures 5.87(c) and 4.45). The roof of the tunnel is turfed over, so blending with the surrounding meadows. The outer edge of the tunnel is planted with shrubs and climbers which hang down over the open section and help to conceal the tunnel from housing on the other side. This side is protected by an absorptive perforated metal barrier. Further along, the tunnel is cut into the hillside and the roof of the tunnel is graded into the surrounding land (see Figure 5.87(d)). From there the land rises more significantly and the tunnel roof becomes part of the greater expanse of farmland (Figure 5.91).

The covering of carriageways is becoming more commonplace in Europe. A further urban example may be found near Hamburg airport, where half of a new motorway link road to the airport is being covered. The roof area has been turned into an amenity zone and the noise mitigation has been enhanced with an earth mound at the edge of the roof. This mound has been provided with irrigation to help the establishment and maintenance of planting (Figure 5.92).

5.91 Galleried tunnel roof tied into the visual character of the surrounding farmland

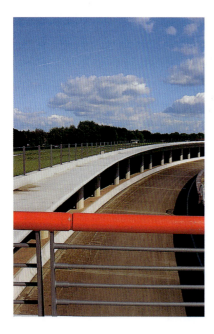

5.92 Galleried tunnel fully obscures views of the motorway from houses (left)

5.93 Unobtrusive escape door with well-designed signage fits in with the overall barrier concept

1.

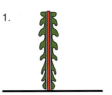

Climbers – close screening
of barrier with self-clinging
species or climbing
wires attached

5.

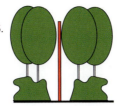

Deciduous trees and shrubs –
increased partial screening

Maintenance zone
may be required
on either side

2.

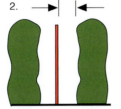

Hedging – formal or informal,
deciduous or evergreen

6.

Planter with planting – adds
height to planting and greater
height to vegetation

3.

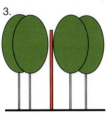

Deciduous trees – partial
screening, more screening
in summer

7.

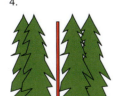

Earth mound adds
height to planting and
greater screening height

4.

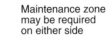

Evergreen trees – most
screening usually
all year round

8.

Combination of differerent types of
planting can give good screening

Note: Planting need not be symmetrical; planting may be formal or
informal; maintenance requirements may require planting to be
some distance away from the face of the barrier.

5.94 Barriers and vegetation

Escape routes

Escape doors and routes should be designed as an integral part of the barrier and should tie in with the overall visual concept. It is important, however, that these routes can be easily distinguished and therefore adequate signage and attention-drawing devices should be used without being obtrusive (Figure 5.93; see also Figure 4.40).

Planting and barriers

Planting is an essential part of environmental design and should be considered in most cases when planning and designing barriers. The planting has a softening, organic effect on an engineered barrier. A planting strategy should be developed with a concept and hierarchy tied into the design of the overall noise and landscape mitigation measures (Figure 5.94).

Planting can be used in many different ways. It may partially hide the barrier, cover it completely, or create focal points. It may be attached to the barrier by climbing wires, frames or ties; be located immediately adjacent to it; or be set back from it at various points where it helps to break up the monotony of the façade. Planting can also be located well away from the barrier, possibly off-site by agreement with the landowner, and this helps to diminish its visual impact (Figure 5.95).

Depending on location and landscape character, planting can be organic and natural, or more formally conceived with geometrically designed rows and avenues, or with planters. Barriers can be specially designed to incorporate shrubs and other vegetation (Figure 5.96). Regular planting schemes along the length of the barrier can serve to co-ordinate and harmonise its appearance.

5.95 Sequential planting helps to break up views to the barrier

5.96 Planting within the barrier planter and adjacent trees help to integrate the barrier into the landscape

5.97 Tree and shrub planting may be effectively located within a narrow planter

When designing planting immediately adjacent to a barrier, care must be taken that the barrier does not cause a rain shadow, restricting the quantity of water reaching the plants' roots. This may be a particular problem with larger cantilevered structures that overhang planted areas. In these situations irrigation is essential.

Planting does not necessarily require huge amounts of space. Climbers, both evergreen and deciduous, can be located within widths of 300 mm if care is taken over soil types and drainage requirements. In urban areas, where space is limited, fastigiate trees, or trees of a narrow habit can be used to advantage (Figures 5.97 and 5.98; see also Figure 5.41).

Well-designed planting is usually a visual asset. It also has the effect of enhancing the soil stability, the microclimate and the wildlife environment.

5.98 Fastigiate trees used as part of the overall barrier design

The mitigation planting strategy and design details should always be agreed with the design team as this may well affect the acoustic mitigation strategy and other environmental issues.

References

1. The Highways Agency (1992) *Design Manual for Roads and Bridges*, Volume 10, Section 5, Part 2 HA66/95 – Environmental barriers: Technical Requirements, HMSO, London.
2. The Highways Agency (1992) *Design Manual for Roads and Bridges*, Volume 10, Section 5, Part 1 HA65/94 – Design Guide for Environmental Barriers, Section 7. HMSO, London.
3. Roads and Traffic Authority of NSW (1991) *Noise Barriers and Catalogue of Selection Possibilities, Part 1, Noise Barriers*, RTA, Haymarket, NSW.
4. Tutt, P. and Adler, D. (Eds) (1985) *New Metric Handbook*, Architectural Press, London.
5. Coppin, N. J. and Richards, I. G. (eds) (1990) *Use of Vegetation in Civil Engineering*, Butterworths and CIRIA (joint pubs.), London, pp. 39–40.

Engineering, safety, environmental and cost considerations

6

Introduction

To be entirely successful, the design of a noise barrier must address all of the relevant environmental, engineering and safety requirements. The design should be led by the noise control objective and should be visually acceptable while not adversely affecting the landscape character and quality. The other issues must be acknowledged throughout the design because, ultimately, statutory and safety considerations will take precedence. Proper provision must also be made in the budget for any barriers that are necessary to meet the design objectives.

The Highways Agency provides advice on these issues.[1] However, the European Committee for Standardization is preparing a standard for the mechanical performance and stability of noise barriers which will harmonise these requirements across Europe.

Engineering considerations

The first part of the proposed European standard will provide criteria for categorising noise barriers into performance classes. Compliance test methods and reporting procedures are defined for the following aspects:

- wind and static loading, including the effects of dynamic loading due to passing vehicles and static loading due to snow on nonvertical barriers;
- self-weight, including the dry weight to allow an estimate of the sound insulation to be made and, where appropriate, the wet weight;
- impact of stones during normal road use;
- safety of a vehicle in collision with a barrier;
- dynamic load from snow clearance.

General safety and environmental considerations are dealt with in the second part of the standard. The aspects covered are:

- resistance to brush fire;
- secondary safety associated with the risk of falling debris after impact;
- environmental protection with the requirement that any risks posed by barrier materials to the environment over time or at disposal are identified;
- means of escape in emergency, which includes access and egress for personnel and vehicles in emergency and for maintenance;
- light reflection;
- transparency.

Secondary safety is of particular importance where barriers are installed on bridges or between carriageways. Where transparent panels are used, they are made shatterproof by either using laminated glass or by embedding thin strands of fibreglass within acrylic sheets. Panels are tied to each other and to the support posts with short lengths of wire rope at each joint or by using a continuous cable along the length of the barrier (Figure 6.1).

Escape doors and routes are standard features in noise barriers, except for the shortest which allow escape at either end. In the UK the Highways Agency requires doors to be provided at intervals of not more than 200 m, and they should be wide enough to allow stretchers to be carried through. The public should be able to open the doors from the roadside in an emergency, but only maintenance staff and emergency services should have access from the rear. Steps or ramps are provided from the carriageway to the door where it is on a cutting or an embankment. Disabled drivers can be catered for by providing gaps with overlaps in the safety fence and the barrier. Vehicle access doors can also be provided for emergency and maintenance vehicles. The acoustic performance of the barrier should not be compromised by the presence of escape routes (Figures 6.2 and 6.3).

The proposed standard does not cover all of the relevant safety and environmental factors and the following should also be considered:

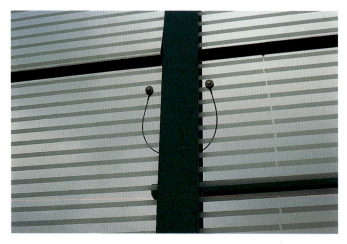

6.1 Panels are tied to each other and the post for secondary safety

6.2 Doors for people and vehicles can be combined for escape and access purposes

- maintaining the required forward visibility lines for drivers;
- avoiding permanent shadow zones that encourage ice formation;
- sustainability – local materials are likely to produce a more harmonious design solution; moreover, their use should be considered to minimise energy costs associated with imported materials. Similarly, local labour should be used wherever possible; the use of materials from non-renewable sources should be avoided.

A further part of the proposed standard will address the long-term durability of barrier materials. The standard will specify test procedures for measuring the resistance to the following agents:

- chemical agents;
- de-icing salts;
- dirty water;
- dew;
- freezing and thawing;
- heat;
- UV light.

Environmental considerations

The construction of an environmental noise barrier may influence a range of environmental issues. These will vary from scheme to scheme and according to the type of barrier used, for example:

- severance – the potential impediment to the existing movement of people or the impediment of existing operations;
- loss of land – the potential loss of agricultural, amenity and other land-use types;

Barrier with escape door

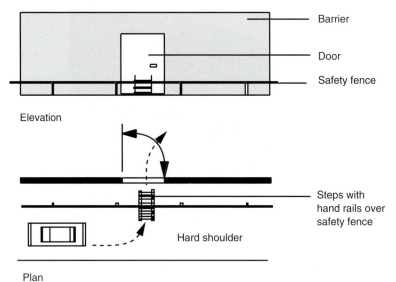

Barrier

Door

Safety fence

Elevation

Steps with
hand rails over
safety fence

Hard shoulder

Plan

Barrier with escape channel – Option 1

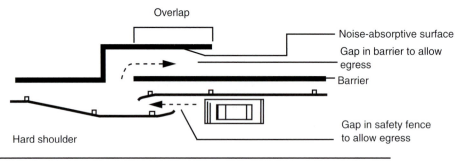

Overlap

Noise-absorptive surface

Gap in barrier to allow
egress

Barrier

Hard shoulder

Gap in safety fence
to allow egress

Plan

Barrier with escape channel – Option 2

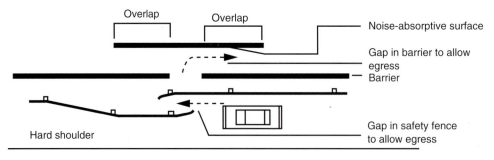

Overlap

Overlap

Noise-absorptive surface

Gap in barrier to allow
egress

Barrier

Hard shoulder

Gap in safety fence
to allow egress

Plan

6.3 Escape doors

- archaeology – the potential impact on existing and unknown sites;
- built heritage – the potential impact on listed buildings, National Trust inalienable land, conservation areas, registered parks and gardens and other designated national, county and local sites;
- nature conservation – severance and disruption of habits and habitat of wildlife, including mammals, birds and invertebrates, by creating obstacles to paths of travel and effects on designated sites such as SSSIs (Sites of Special Scientific Interest);
- local hydrology – the potential disruption to water bodies and drainage patterns with potential effects on the existing ecology;
- driver stress – the potential impacts on travellers.

Each issue and the potential land-take should be considered separately with the relevant environmental specialist.

The design of a barrier may in fact have some positive effect on the environment and noise barriers may be used to fulfil other environmental objectives. For example, an earth mound may be constructed to fulfil nature conservation objectives to provide a habitat for wildlife. Vertical screens can be used as part of a nature conservation strategy to stop deer, badgers and other wildlife from straying onto the traffic corridor and to direct them to wildlife bridges or tunnels.

Costs

Cost is probably the main factor that has determined the type and visual character of barriers found in the UK. This, however, does not appear to be the case in Europe, where visual integration and landscape quality considerations are given greater weight. Methods need to be devised to acknowledge the true value of maintaining environmental quality if barriers are to be part of a cost–benefit analysis. If a value is not given to achieving environmental objectives, only the cheapest and inappropriate solutions will be provided.

In most cases barriers have been chosen due to their comparative material costs. The Highways Agency[2] provides a list of comparative costs and maintenance implications (Table 6.1). This table attempts to provide information in a simple form. It must be remembered, however, that the location of any barrier will affect the cost of any particular type of barrier. Moreover, the full construction costs can significantly alter the relative barrier costs.

Although it is helpful for budgetary purposes to know what the costs of barrier types are, the budget for each barrier must include all those items necessary to meet the environmental objectives:

- the barrier itself with all its design elements;
- barrier supports and foundations;
- purchase of land for the barrier;
- purchase of land for landscape and other environmental purposes;

Table 6.1 Maintenance cost indicators

Barrier type	Factors taken into consideration	Relative cost
Earth mound	grass cutting, planting maintenance	fairly low
Timber screen	inspection/repair, periodic treatment	low
Concrete screen	inspection/repair, periodic cleaning	very low
Brickwork wall	inspection/repair, periodic cleaning/ repointing	very low
Plastic/planted system	inspection/repair, periodic cleaning, planting maintenance, irrigation	moderate
Metal panels	inspection/repair, repainting/ treatment, tighten bolts, check earthing	fairly low
Absorbent panels	inspection/repair, periodic cleaning	fairly low
Transparent panels	inspection/repair, regular cleaning/ treatment	fairly high
Crib wall	inspection/repair	low

- soiling and grading of land;
- planting;
- the installation of irrigation.

An adequate maintenance budget must also be provided to ensure that the landscape and environmental objectives are met. This may vary depending on the type of barrier required.

References

1. The Highways Agency (1992) *Design Manual for Roads and Bridges*, Volume 10, Environmental Barriers, Section 5, Environmental Barriers, HMSO, London.
2. The Highways Agency (1992) *Design Manual for Roads and Bridges*, Volume 10, Environmental Barriers, Section 5, Part 2 Environmental Barriers: Technical Requirements, HMSO, London, p. 9/3.

Appendix 1 - Index of manufacturers, installers and suppliers

COMPANY NAME	Design/consultancy	Manufacture	Supply	Installation	Absorptive brick–clay/concrete/stone	Absorptive sheet metal (A=aluminium S=steel)	Absorptive timber	Absorptive concrete (woodfibre/granular)	Transparent – glass	Transparent – acrylic sheet	Reflective timber	Reflective concrete	Reflective brick ceramic/aluminium/steel	Plastic	Solar panels	Devon banks	Gabions	Bio-barrier: concrete stack/crib system	Bio-barrier: timber stack/crib system	Bio-barrier: geotextile earth retention system	Bio-barrier: box system	Bio-barrier: woven–willow system
Akustik & Lyd Plinius & Co. – Copenhagen, Denmark	●					A/S			●						●							
ARC Concrete Ltd		●		●									●									
Baco Contracts	●	●	●	●		A			●													
Boral Edenhall Concrete Products Ltd		●	●	●								●										
Buffalo Structures	●	●	●	●							●											
Comtec (UK) Ltd	●		●	●														●	●	●		
Ecometal		●	●			S																
E C Environmental Systems Ltd	●		●	●			●	●			●											
Grass Concrete International Ltd	●		●																			
Grodan	●		●																			
GSB (Holdings) plc	●	●	●	●							●											●
ICI Acrylics		●	●							●												
Industrial Acoustics Company Ltd						A/S																
Lionweld Kennedy		●	●	●	●																	
Maccaferri Ltd	●		●	●													●			●		
Pilkington United Kingdom Ltd		●	●						●													
Radian Acoustics	●		●		●	A	●	●			●	●	●									
Rhom Ltd		●	●							●												
Royston Steel Fencing Ltd	●	●	●	●	●		●	●	●	●	●						●				●	
Sound Absorption Ltd		●	●	●							●	●										
Stenoak Fencing and Construction Ltd				●			●	●	●	●	●	●										
Tinsley Wire Ltd	●	●	●													●	●					
Torvale Building Products			●				●															
Tubosider UK Ltd	●	●	●	●							●											●
Urbis Acoustic Products	●		●	●		A			●	●					●							
Van Campen Bending Techniques BV		●	●	●	●								●									

Company addresses

Akustik & Lyd Plinius & Co. ApS
Symbion Science Park Copenhagen
Fruebjergvej 3
DK 2100 Copenhagen
Denmark
Tel: +45 39 17 97 50
Fax: +45 39 29 00 99

ARC Concrete Ltd
PO Box 14
Appleford Road
Sutton Courtenay
Abingdon
Oxfordshire
OX14 4UB
Tel: 01235 848808
Fax: 01235 847284

Baco Contracts
Chalfont Park
Gerrards Cross
Buckinghamshire
SL9 0QB
Tel: 01753 233200
Fax: 01753 233445

Boral Edenhall Concrete Products Ltd
Barbary Plains
Edenhall
Penrith
Cumbria
CA11 8SP
Tel: 01768 890202
Fax: 01768 881494

Buffalo Structures
Ipsden
Wallingford
Oxfordshire
OX10 6BS
Tel: 01491 838368
Fax: 01491 825418

Comtec (UK) Ltd
Bells Yew Green
Tunbridge Wells
Kent
TN3 9BQ
Tel: 01892 750664
Fax: 01892 750660
Email: comtec@comtec-uk.co.uk

Ecometal
245 Govan Road
Glasgow
G51 2SQ
Tel: 0141 427 7000
Fax: 0141 427 5345

EC Environmental Systems Ltd
Suite 210
Grovesnor House
Central Park
Telford
Shropshire
TF2 9TW
Tel: 01952 292824
Fax: 01952 201214

Grass Concrete International Ltd
Walker House
22 Bond Street
Wakefield
West Yorkshire
WF1 2QP
Tel: 01924 379443
Fax: 01924 290289

Grodan
Grodania
Wern Tarw
Pencoed
Bridgend
Mid Glamorgan
CF35 6NY
Tel: 01656 863853/611
Fax: 01656 863853/611

GSB (Holdings) plc
Surrey House
39/41 High Street
Newmarket
Suffolk
CB8 8NA
Tel: 01638 668196
Fax: 01638 668204

ICI Acrylics
PO Box 34
Darwen
Lancashire
BB3 1QB
Tel: 01254 874444
Fax: 01254 873300

Industrial Acoustics Company Ltd
IAC House
Moorside Road
Winchester
Hampshire
SO23 7US
Tel: 01962 873000
Fax: 01962 873132

Lionweld Kennedy Ltd
Marsh Road
Middlesborough
TS1 5JS
Tel: 01642 245151
Fax: 01642 224710
Email: sales@lkltd.vector-steel.co.uk

Maccaferri Ltd
Leyden Road
Stevenage
Hertfordshire
SG1 2BP
Tel: 01438 315504
Fax: 01438 740335

Pilkington United Kingdom Ltd
Prescot Road
St Helens
WA10 3TT
Tel: 01744 692000
Fax: 01744 613049

Radian Acoustics
Market Place
Wymondham
Norwich
NR18 0AR
Tel: 01953 603255
Fax: 01953 601319

Rohm Ltd
Plastics Division
Bradbourne Drive
Tilbrook
Milton Keynes
MK7 8AU
Tel: 01908 274414
Fax: 01908 274588

Royston Steel Fencing Ltd
Tadlow Road
Tadlow
Royston
Hertfordshire
SG8 0EP
Tel: 01767 631721
Fax: 01767 631637

Sound Absorption Ltd
Broadclough Works
Burnley Road
Bacup
Lancashire
OL13 8PJ
Tel: 01706 213477
Fax: 01706 214147

Stenoak Fencing and Construction Company Ltd
Stenoak House
New Town
Uckfield
East Sussex
TN22 5DL
Tel: 01825 762266
Fax: 01825 765432

Tinsley Wire (Sheffield) Ltd
Gridweld Division
Woodhouse Lane
Wigan
WN6 7NS
Tel: 01942 244071
Fax: 01942 824573

Torvale Building Products
Pembridge
Leominster
Herefordshire
HR6 9LA
Tel: 01544 388262
Fax: 01544 388568

Tubosider United Kingdom Ltd
24 Kingsland Grange
Woolston
Cheshire
WA1 4RW
Tel: 01925 820900
Fax: 01925 820990

Urbis Acoustic Products
1 Telford Road
Houndmills
Basingstoke
RG21 2YW
Tel: 01256 354446
Fax: 01256 841314

Van Campen Bending Techniques BV
15 Wrose Avenue
Swain House
Bradford
Yorkshire
BD2 1HP
Tel: 01274 671111
Fax: 01274 671122

Author index

Subject index

Bold text refers to figures, italic text to tables